D1222341

At Issue

|The Wealth Divide

Other Books in the At Issue Series:

At Issue

I The Wealth Divide

Noël Merino, Book Editor

GREENHAVEN PRESS
A part of Gale, Cengage Learning

GALE
CENGAGE Learning·

Farmington Hills, Mich • San Francisco • New York • Waterville, Maine
Meriden, Conn • Mason, Ohio • Chicago

Patricia Coryell, *Vice President & Publisher, New Products & GVRL*
Douglas Dentino, *Manager, New Products*
Judy Galens, *Acquisitions Editor*

For more information, contact:
Greenhaven Press
27500 Drake Rd.
Farmington Hills, MI 48331-3535
Or you can visit our Internet site at gale.cengage.com

For product information and technology assistance, contact us at

Gale Customer Support, 1-800-877-4253
For permission to use material from this text or product, submit all requests online at www.cengage.com/permissions

Further permissions questions can be e-mailed to permissionrequest@cengage.com

Articles in Greenhaven Press anthologies are often edited for length to meet page requirements. In addition, original titles of these works are changed to clearly present the main thesis and to explicitly indicate the author's opinion. Every effort is made to ensure that Greenhaven Press accurately reflects the original intent of the authors. Every effort has been made to trace the owners of copyrighted material.

LIBRARY OF CONGRESS CATALOGING-IN-PUBLICATION DATA

The wealth divide / Noël Merino, book editor.
    pages cm. -- (At issue)
    Includes bibliographical references and index.
    ISBN 978-0-7377-7197-8 (hardcover) -- ISBN 978-0-7377-7198-5 (pbk.)
    1. Income distribution--United States. 2. Rich people--United States. 3. Poor--United States. 4. Equality--United States. I. Merino, Noël, editor.
    HC110.E5W43 2015
    339.2'20973--dc23
                                                2014029438

Printed in the United States of America
1 2 3 4 5 6 7 18 17 16 15 14

Contents

Introduction

According to a 2013 report by Credit Suisse Global, the average wealth per adult in the world reached $51,600 in 2013. But the global wealth divide is severe: the top 10 percent of the world population owns 86 percent of global wealth, whereas the bottom half of adults owns barely 1 percent of global wealth. In the United States, there also exists a wealth divide. According to Credit Suisse Global, the average wealth of a US adult in 2013 was $301,140, but the median individual wealth of $44,911 (the amount at which 50 percent of individuals have more and 50 percent have less) hints at the extent to which wealth is not equally shared across the US population.

A report from the US Census Bureau by Alfred Gottschalck, Marina Vornovytskyy, and Adam Smith measures the median household net worth: the total assets of households (rather than individuals) minus any outstanding debt. According to the authors, median household net worth in the United States in 2011 was $68,828. A large portion of household wealth in the United States exists in the form of home equity—the value of one's home minus the amount still owed. Excluding home equity, average household wealth in 2011 was $16,942, which includes such assets as savings accounts, retirement accounts, motor vehicles, and businesses (but excluding home furnishings and jewelry).

G. William Domhoff, a professor of sociology at University of California, Santa Cruz, reports data on household net worth by percentiles. Breaking US households down into brackets according to the size of household net worth, he claims that the top 1 percent of households in 2010 had an average net worth of $16,439,400, and the top 20 percent had an average household net worth of $2,061,600. However, he claims that the bottom 40 percent actually had an average household net worth of −$10,600, meaning that on average their debts outweighed any assets held. He contends that in 2010 the top 20 percent of households in the United States owned 89 percent of all privately held wealth (with the top 1 percent accounting for 35 percent of all wealth), leaving 11 percent of total wealth for the bottom 80 percent of US households.

Wealth is related to income, as income is one way to build wealth, but data about income do not capture differences in wealth created by inheritance and investments from past income. The Pew Research Center reports that the median income of US households in 2010 was $59,127. Dividing households into three income groups, Pew reports that in 2010 upper-income households had median income of $161,252, middle-income households had median income of $69,487, and lower-income households had median income of $23,063. Pew claims that whereas upper-income households comprised only 20 percent of US adults, the income in this group accounted for almost half (46 percent) of all US income. By contrast, lower-income households made up 29 percent of all US adults but only 9 percent of aggregate income.

A Pew Research Center survey conducted in 2011 found that Americans are concerned about the wealth divide in the United States. Almost two-thirds of the population (66 percent) believes that there are "very strong" or "strong" conflicts between the rich and the poor. A separate 2011 Pew Research Center survey found that 61 percent of Americans believe that the US economic system unfairly favors the wealthy. However, the American public is divided about the importance of narrowing the wealth gap between the rich and the poor. In a 2011 Gallup poll, when asked how important it was for the federal government to enact policies to reduce the income and wealth gap between the rich and the poor, 28 percent said it was "not important," 26 percent said it was "somewhat important," 29 percent said it was "very important," and 17 percent said it was "extremely important."

Opposing viewpoints exist not only about what to do about the wealth divide but also about how to measure wealth and income. While no one would argue that there is no wealth inequality in the United States, there are conflicting accounts about the extent of the inequality. Regardless, there is wide-ranging debate about whether or not this divide is a problem. Furthermore, among those who think that the wealth gap should be reduced, there are competing views about how it should be addressed and whether or not the government should play a role. These fascinating and competing views about the inequality of wealth and income in the United States are explored in *At Issue: The Wealth Divide*.

1

The Wealth Divide Between Rich and Poor Harms the US Economy

Jonathan Rauch

Jonathan Rauch is a contributing editor for The Atlantic *and* National Journal.

There is an emerging economic view among progressives that inequality has reached damaging levels, which is contrary to the dominant mainstream economic view of the last few decades that inequality is economically neutral. New evidence, however, supports the view that extreme inequality is damaging to the economy because it suppresses growth and creates a risky credit bubble. As a result, the era of dismissing the issue of inequality is coming to an end.

At a salon dinner in Washington recently, the subject was inequality. An economist took the floor. Economic inequality, he said, is not a problem. Poverty is a problem, certainly. Unemployment, yes. Slow growth, yes. But he had never yet seen a good reason to believe that inequality, as such—the widening gap between top and bottom, as distinct from poverty or stagnation—is harmful to the economy.

Perhaps he spoke too soon.

The Emerging Criticism of Inequality

Once in a while, a new economic narrative gives renewed strength to an old political ideology. Two generations ago, supply-side economics transformed conservatism's case against big government from a merely ideological claim to an economic one. After decades in which Keynesians had dismissed conservatism as an economic dead end ("Hooverism"), supply-siders turned the tables. The Right could argue that reducing spending and (especially) tax rates was a matter not merely of political preference but of economic urgency.

Something potentially analogous is stirring among the Left. An emerging view holds that inequality has reached levels that are damaging not only to liberals' sense of justice but to the economy's stability and growth. If this narrative catches on, it could give the egalitarian Left new purchase in the national economic debate.

"Widely unequal societies do not function efficiently, and their economies are neither stable nor sustainable in the long term," Joseph E. Stiglitz, a Nobel Prize-winning economist, writes in his new book, *The Price of Inequality*. "Taken to its extreme—and this is where we are now—this trend distorts a country and its economy as much as the quick and easy revenues of the extractive industry distort oil- or mineral-rich countries."

For years, the idea that inequality, per se, is economically neutral has been the mainstream view not just among conservatives but among most Americans.

Stiglitz's formulation is a good two-sentence summary of the emerging macroeconomic indictment of inequality, and the two key words in his second sentence, "extreme" and "distort," make good handles for grasping the arguments. Let's consider them in turn.

The Promise of Inequality

Equality and Efficiency: The Big Trade-off was a 1975 book written by the late Arthur Okun, a Harvard Unversity economist and pillar of the economic establishment. Okun's title encapsulated an economic consensus: Inequality is the price America pays for a dynamic, efficient economy; we may not like it, but the alternatives are worse. As long as the bottom and the middle are moving up, there is no reason to mind if the top is moving up faster, except perhaps for an ideological grudge against the rich—what conservatives call the politics of envy.

For years, the idea that inequality, per se, is economically neutral has been the mainstream view not just among conservatives but among most Americans outside the further reaches of the political Left. There might be ideological or ethical reasons to object to a growing gap between the rich and the rest. But economic reasons? No.

"The debate for many years looked settled," said Robert Shapiro, an economist with Sonecon, a Washington consulting firm. "Changes in the economy and changes in the data have reopened the debate."

Economists know more today than they did in Okun's day about the distribution of income. "There's been enormous progress in measuring inequality—Nobel Prize-level progress," said David Moss, an economist at Harvard Business School. As the data came in and the view got clearer, the picture that emerged was unsettling.

"In the 1990s," Moss said, "it began to appear that income was being concentrated among the very highest earners and that stagnation was occurring not just at the low end but across most income levels." It wasn't just that the top was doing better than the rest, but that the very top was absorbing most of the economy's growth. This was a more extreme and dynamic kind of inequality than the country was accustomed to.

According to a recent Congressional Budget Office report, those in the top 1 percent of households doubled their share of pretax income from 1979 to 2007; the bottom 80 percent saw their share fall. Worse, while the average income for the top 1 percent more than tripled (after inflation), the bottom 80 percent saw only feeble income growth, on the order of just 20 percent over nearly 30 years. The rising tide was raising a few boats hugely and most other boats not very much.

It thus began to seem that the old bargain, in which inequality bought rising incomes for all, had failed—much as the Keynesian bargain (bigger government, faster growth) had failed two generations earlier. "The majority of Americans have simply not been benefiting from the country's growth," Stiglitz wrote, overstating things—but not by a lot.

The Impact of Inequality

So much for "extreme." Next came the financial-system meltdown of 2008 and the Great Recession, which bring us to "distort"—how an excess of inequality may have warped the economy.

As the data on inequality came in, economists noticed something else: The last time inequality rose to its current heights was in the late 1920s, just before a financial meltdown. Might there be a connection? In 2010, Moss plotted inequality and bank failures since 1864 on the same graph; he found an eerily close fit. That is, in both the 1920s and the first decade of this century, inequality and financial crisis went hand in glove. Others noticed the same conjunction. Although Moss recognized that a simple correlation based on only two examples proves nothing, he wasn't alone in wondering if something might be going on. But what?

Income inequality can exert a significant drag on effective demand.

Different economists suggest different pathways by which inequality at the microeconomic level might cause macroeconomic problems. What follows is a composite story based on common elements.

As with supply-side, the case starts with the two extreme ends or a curve. Supply-siders pointed out that two tax rates produce no revenue: zero percent and 100 percent. Inequality traces an analogous curve. At both extremes of inequality—either perfect inequality, where a single person receives all the income, or perfect equality, where rewards end incentives cannot exist—an economy won't function. So, Moss said, "the question is: Where are the break points in between?"

Suppose various changes (globalization, technology, increased demand for skills, deregulation, financial innovation, the rising premium on superstar talent—take your pick) drove most of the economy's income gains to the few people at the top. The rich save—that is, invest—15 to 25 percent of their income, Stiglitz writes, whereas those on the lower rungs consume most or all of their income and save little or nothing. As the country's earnings migrate toward the highest reaches of the income distribution, therefore, you would expect to see the economy's mix of activity tip away from spending (demand) and toward investment.

That is fine up to a point, but beyond that, imbalances may arise. As Christopher Brown, an economist at Arkansas State University, put it in a pioneering 2004 paper, "Income inequality can exert a significant drag on effective demand." Looking back on the two decades before 1986, Brown found that if the gap between rich and poor hadn't grown wider, consumption spending would have been almost 12 percent higher than it actually was. That was a big enough number to have produced a noticeable macroeconomic impact. Stiglitz, in his book, argues that an inequality-driven shift away from consumption accounts for "the entire shortfall in aggregate demand—and hence in the U.S. economy—today."

True, saving and spending should eventually re-equilibrate. But "eventually" can be a long time. Meanwhile, extreme and growing inequality might depress demand enough to deepen and prolong a downturn, perhaps even turning it into a lost decade—or two.

The Availability of Easy Credit

So inequality might suppress growth. It might also cause instability. In a democracy, politicians and the public are unlikely to accept depressed spending power if they can help it. They can try to compensate by easing credit standards, effectively encouraging the non-rich to sustain purchasing power by borrowing. They might, for example, create policies allowing banks to write flimsy home mortgages and encouraging consumers to seek them. Call this the "let them eat credit" strategy.

For decades, more than half of the increase in the country's GDP poured into the bank accounts of the richest Americans.

"Cynical as it may seem," Raghuram Rajan, a finance professor at the University of Chicago's Booth School of Business, wrote in his 2010 book, *Fault Lines: How Hidden Fractures Still Threaten the World Economy*, "easy credit has been used as a palliative throughout history by governments that are unable to address the deeper anxieties of the middle class directly." That certainly seems to have happened in the years leading to the mortgage crisis. Marianne Bertrand and Adair Morse, also of Chicago's business school, have found that legislators who represent constituencies with higher inequality are more likely to support the easing of credit. Several papers by International Monetary Fund [IMF] economists comparing countries likewise find support for the "let them eat credit" approach. And credit splurges, they find, bring on instability and current-account deficits.

You can see where the logic leads. The economy, propped up on shaky credit, becomes more vulnerable to shocks. When a recession comes, the economy takes a double hit as banks fail and credit-fueled consumer spending collapses. That is not a bad description of what happened in the 1920s and again during these past few years. "When—as appears to have happened in the long run-up to both crises—the rich lend a large part of their added income to the poor and middle class, and when income inequality grows for several decades," the IMF's Michael Kumhot and Romain Rancière wrote, "debt-to-income ratios increase sufficiently to raise the risk of a major crisis."

But wait. Which is it? Does inequality depress demand? Or does it inflate credit bubbles that maintain demand? Unfortunately, the answer can be both. If inequality is severe enough, there could be enough of it to cause the country to inflate a dangerous credit bubble and still not offset the reduction in demand.

And, no, we're not finished. Inequality may also be destabilizing in another way. "Of every dollar of real income growth that was generated between 1976 and 2007," Rajan wrote, "58 cents went to the top 1 percent of households." In other words, for decades, more than half of the increase in the country's GDP [gross domestic product] poured into the bank accounts of the richest Americans, who needed liquid investments in which to put their additional wealth. Their appetite for new investment vehicles fueled a surge in what Arkansas State's Brown calls "financial engineering"—the concoction of exotic financial instruments, which acted on the financial sector like steroids.

Those changes, the French economists Jean-Paul Fitoussi and Francesco Saraceno wrote in a 2010 paper, "help explain why the expansion of the financial sector was so out of touch with the economy. And why, for example, in the U.S., the financial sector represented about 40 percent of the total profit of the economy." Alas, when the recession struck, the financial sector's gigantism and complexity helped turn what might have been a brush fire into a meltdown.

The Case Against Inequality

In the 1970s, supply-siders argued that tax rates had become high enough to choke off growth and destabilise the economy.

Today's rethink makes the same kind of case against inequality. "Some inequality is a good thing in terms of establishing incentives to pursue arduous career paths," economist Brown conceded in an interview. "But it's been taken to such an extreme that it has become a major economic problem and a huge social problem."

With the arguable exception of Stiglitz, the new macroegalitarians are modest in their claims. Most acknowledge that much work needs to be done to tease out cause and effect. Most also reject remedies that rely on aggressive redistribution. Instead, they emphasize measures, such as better education and training, that attempt to raise the bottom and middle rather than to bring down the top. In comparison with many of the supply-siders, these guys are recklessly responsible.

At a minimum, however, they have found smoke, and there has certainly been a fire. The era when Washington economists and politicians could dismiss inequality as a second- or third-tier issue may be ending. And progressives, potentially, have a case against inequality that might put accusations of "class warfare" and "politics of envy" behind them.

2

A Cell Phone in Every Pot

Aparna Mathur

Aparna Mathur is an economist and resident scholar at the American Enterprise Institute, where she writes about taxes and wages.

Although inequality has increased over the last few decades, people across the wealth spectrum are actually better off than they used to be. Measuring consumption rather than income shows that inequality has not increased as much as it appears when looking only at income. In addition, data about household appliance use shows that Americans have actually experienced a growth in living standards over the last few decades.

Commenting on the state of the economy at a Habitat for Humanity construction site in Oakland, Calif., former president Jimmy Carter recently said that "the disparity between rich people and poor people in America has increased dramatically" and that "the middle class has become more like poor people than they were 30 years ago." These sentiments are commonly echoed across the country as the effects of the most damaging economic slump since the Depression continue into their sixth year.

The Census Bureau's "Income and Poverty" report, released in September, underscored that the economic recovery has largely failed to reach the poor and middle class. However, there is a subtle but substantive difference between stating that *inequality* is worse today than it was 30 years ago, and that *people* are worse off today than they were 30 years ago. Rising inequality does not preclude an improvement in standards of living at the bottom of the income distribution.

Stepping back from the traditional debate about income inequality, Kevin Hassett and I recently co-authored a study that focuses on changes in material standards of living over the last 30 years. Consumption of goods and services is often a far better measure of household welfare than is income. What we buy and consume with our income directly adds to our utility and happiness, and it also has a direct impact on our standard of living.

Several factors add to the attractiveness of using consumption rather than income as a measure of welfare. First, people are able to maintain a steady rate of consumption over their lifetime, while they are obviously less able to have a stable income over a lifetime. Incomes may be exceptionally low when people are very young or very old, and high during the prime working-age years, but individuals can maintain steady consumption and standards of living by borrowing in low-income periods and saving in high-income periods. Second, household income varies greatly depending on how we measure and define it. The much-cited inequality data constructed by economists Thomas Piketty and Emmanuel Saez use pre-tax, pre-transfer income data from the tax records of filers and include realized capital gains. Richard Burkhauser, on the other hand, argues that the true measure of income should focus on the Haig-Simons definition of income: We need to include accrued capital gains on housing and other wealth along with earnings and transfer incomes to get at what people actually think of as income. The CBO provides a post-tax and post-transfers definition of income but does not include accrued capital gains. Depending upon the measure used, analysts reach widely differing conclusions about the state of income inequality. Consumption is easier to understand as a concept, and while we can debate how best to measure it, too, economists have arguably reached more of a consensus about what constitutes consumption for a typical household.

In our study, we used data from the Consumer Expenditure Survey (CEX) and the Residential Energy Consumption Survey (RECS). The CEX provides a good overview of consumption of "nondurables" by American households. In 1984, households in the top income quintile accounted for 37 percent of total expenditures, while households in the bottom quintile accounted for 10 percent. Hence the ratio of top to bottom consumption was approximately 3.7:1. In 2010, that ratio increased to 4.4:1. On average, over the entire period, the ratio is 4.3:1 with a standard deviation of 0.22. Therefore, using this measure, we find that consumption inequality has increased only marginally over time. The gap was widest in 2005, when the share of consumption for the top was 39 percent relative to 8 percent at the bottom, or 4.9:1. In the recent recession, it appears that households at the bottom increased their share by 1 percentage point, relative to their 2005 share, while the share for the top either declined or remained steady. In the 2001 recession, the ratio declined as well, suggesting that recessions tend to foster a more even distribution.

In general, we find that people at all income levels now have access to many more material possessions than they did in the 1980s.

While the CEX provides a good overview of nondurables consumption, it is not a good source of data on the consumption of durable goods. We therefore worked with the RECS data as well. This survey has questions, for instance, on household use of appliances such as microwaves, dishwashers, computers, and printers. What we find is that the access of low-income Americans—those earning less than $20,000 in real 2009 dollars—to devices that are part of the "good life" has increased. The percentage of low-income households with a computer rose from 19.8 percent to 47.7 percent in 2001. The percentage of low-income homes with six or more rooms (excluding bathrooms) rose from 21.9 percent to 30 percent over the same period.

In terms of appliances, the percentage of low-income homes with air-conditioning equipment rose from 65.8 percent to 83.5 percent; with dishwashers from 17.6 percent to 30.8 percent; with a washing machine from 57.2 percent to 62.4 percent; and with a clothes dryer from 44.9 percent to 56.5 percent.

The percentage of low-income households with microwave ovens grew from 74.9 percent to 92.4 percent between 2001 and 2009. Fully 75.5 percent of low-income Americans now have a cell phone, and over a quarter of those have access to the Internet through their phones.

In general, we find that people at all income levels now have access to many more material possessions than they did in the 1980s. Moreover, there has been a narrowing of the gap between high- and low-income classes in terms of owning these items. It's hard to argue that these trends do not represent an improvement in the standard of living. Yet, over a similar period, the standard income dataset for households, the Current Population Survey, shows that the ratio of pre-tax incomes at the top quintile to those in the bottom quintile rose from 11:1 to 15.4:1. Hence the rise in income inequality has coincided with the rise in consumption levels at the bottom.

Whether the explanation for improvement in living standards lies in redistributionist policies and the growth of the safety net, or in technological improvements that have allowed prices of electronics and other durable goods to drop enough so that lower-income households can afford them, or in real improvements in productivity and wages, the bottom line is this: People are better off today than they were 30 years ago.

The typical low-income household today possesses many more appliances and gadgets—items that have traditionally been considered the preserve of the rich—than at any time in history.

Former president Carter seems to grasp the importance of this argument. In the same interview, he said, "The richest people in America would be better off if everybody lived in a decent home and had a chance to pay for it, and if everyone had enough income, even if they had a daily job, to be good buyers for the products that are produced." Seems like we are on the right track, even if it is a long road ahead.

3

Income Inequality Causes Serious Social Ills and Should Be Reduced

Thomas L. Hungerford

Thomas L. Hungerford is senior economist and director of tax and budget policy at the Economic Policy Institute.

Income inequality has risen significantly in the past thirty years. Competitive market forces may help explain the increasing incomes of those at the top, but inequality of capital income and tax policy also are causes of increased inequality. These income disparities can cause increased poverty, reduced social cohesion, and other social ills. Inequality needs to be reduced by altering tax policy, macroeconomic policy, labor market policy, and human capital investments.

It has been fairly well established that U.S. income inequality has been rising significantly over the past 30 years after an extended period of a fairly stable distribution of income. The share of income accruing to the top one percent has increased by more than 10 percentage points—from 9 percent in 1976 to 20 percent by 2011. Inequality of after-tax after-transfer income as measured by the Gini coefficient increased by 33 percent over the same period. It is unlikely that such a rapid and significant rise in inequality has not affected the well-being of the majority of Americans.

Reactions on the right have been varied. Some argue that income inequality is nothing to worry about because of high income or social mobility—a point made by Milton Friedman over 50 years ago. However, research has shown that U.S. intra-generational income mobility has not been particularly great and may have decreased over the past four decades—chances of moving up in the income distribution are not particularly great. The so-called "Great Gatsby curve" shows that there is a negative relationship between inequality and inter-generational mobility. The U.S. with high income inequality has low intergenerational mobility: the apple does not appear to fall far from the tree in the U.S. This all suggests that income inequality is, indeed, something to worry about.

The inflation-adjusted U.S. minimum wage is about 30 percent lower now than it was in the mid-1960s and U.S. unionization rates have been declining since the 1960s.

Others deny that income inequality has risen. The more sophisticated among the deniers cite research by Richard Burkhauser and colleagues who try to examine inequality trends using their version of the more theoretically grounded Haig-Simons definition of income (consumption plus additions to wealth). They find that the "observed growth in income inequality across the distribution" is dramatically reduced, especially the rise in income at the top. Implementing the Haig-Simons income definition, however, requires making several critical assumptions and decisions on what should be included and excluded in the income measure. I suspect their findings are due more to their specific assumptions and exclusions than to real changes in the control over the uses of resources. Research by Edward Wolff and colleagues suggests this may very well be the case. For example, accrued capital gains are difficult to measure especially for sparsely traded assets. Additionally, a full accounting of consumption would include consumption of home-produced goods and services as well as publicly provided goods and services, both of which are difficult to measure.

The Causes of Rising Income Inequality

A great deal of effort has been expended researching the causes of the 30-year increase in U.S. income disparities to find the "smoking gun." One explanation that some claim is the smoking gun is the skill-biased technological change hypothesis— stories based on the supply and demand for skills. In these stories, those at the top of the income distribution have unique talents that are in short supply and command a premium in a market of increasing demand for these talents. Consequently, the earned income of those at the top increases relative to the earnings of those lower down in the distribution and earnings inequality rises. Greg Mankiw calls this the "just deserts perspective" on inequality in his embrace and defense of the top one percent. In other words, rising inequality is the result of competitive market forces.

But this is not the only explanation that has been offered and other explanations are needed to explain the U.S. trend and the differing experiences with income inequality in other countries. Not only has earnings inequality increased, but also inequality of capital income. Additionally, capital income has become a larger share in total income over the past two decades and the correlation between capital income and earnings has also increased, which explains much of the increase in inequality between 1996 and 2006.

Tax policy has also changed with the top tax rates on both ordinary income and capital gains falling, and the tax system becoming less progressive. This change in tax policy is part of the change in institutions or rules affecting income. The inflation-adjusted U.S. minimum wage is about 30 percent lower now than it was in the mid-1960s and U.S. unionization rates have been declining since the 1960s. Jacob Hacker and Paul Pierson argue that policy-makers have changed the rules of the American economy to benefit the few at the expense of the many. The increasing use of stock options over this time to align corporate manager interests with shareholder interests rather than with stakeholders (i.e., workers, customers, local community and shareholder) interests may have further contributed to rent-seeking behavior. All of these institutional changes have increased the gains to bargaining and rent extraction by CEOs [chief executive officers], managers, and others with bargaining power.

The Consequences of Rising Income Inequality

Large and growing income disparities have been linked to various social ills. First, if the income gains of those at the top come at the expense of those lower in the income distribution, then poverty could increase as individuals are pushed down in the distribution and the income of some is pushed below the poverty threshold. The poverty rate in the U.S. has increased between 1979 and 2007 from 11.7 percent to 12.5 percent before rising to 15.0 percent by 2011. Further evidence of the top's income gains coming at the expense of those lower in the distribution is the trend in labor productivity growth and average hourly compensation growth of production and non-supervisory workers (about 80 percent of the private sector workforce). The two tracked each other quite closely until the late 1970s. Since then, labor productivity has continued to grow (by almost 90 percent) while average hourly compensation has largely been stagnant. If most workers are not benefiting from productivity growth, then who is?

Second, rising income inequality could reduce social cohesion. The wide-spread but all-too-short-lived Occupy Wall Street movement could be one manifestation of the reduction in social cohesion. Additionally, a 2011 Pew Research Center survey shows that a majority of Americans (66 percent) think there are strong conflicts between the rich and the poor.

A large and growing body of research has shown a link between income inequality and health/longevity disparities.

Third and closely related is the political powerlessness of poor and middle-income Americans. Individuals at the top of the income distribution influence the political process through generous campaign contributions, lobbying, and the revolving door between government employment and the private sector. It has been shown that policy outcomes often reflect the preferences of the most affluent rather of those lower down in the income distribution.

Fourth, the well-being of the middle-class could be affected by rising inequality. The consumption of positional goods, which are goods whose value depends on how they compare with things owned by others, by high-income individuals could lead to increased expenditures by middle class individuals as they try to "keep up with the Joneses." In other words, a positional goods expenditure arms race ensues, which is inefficient as well as welfare reducing.

Lastly, large income disparities can be hazardous to health. A large and growing body of research has shown a link between income inequality and health/longevity disparities: the larger the income disparities the steeper the health gradient and the larger the gap in mortality rates between rich and poor.

The Solutions to Rising Income Inequality

Since there are many causes of the significant rise in income inequality, several policies will likely be needed to reduce income inequality to manageable levels. I am not proposing the complete elimination of income inequality, but rather reducing it to a point that minimizes the deleterious effects of inequality and yet maintains the incentives for hard work and risk-taking. I will limit my discussion to four sets of policies that I think are particularly important.

Tax Policy. Changes in tax policy over the past few decades were an important contributor to rising income inequality and are, therefore, a critical piece to reducing income inequality. The dramatic decline in the top statutory tax rate—from 91 percent in the 1950s to 35 percent in the 2000s (recently increased to 39.6 percent)—provided an incentive to those with power to increase their income through rent seeking. Many would argue that returning to a 91 percent top tax rate is neither desirable nor feasible. But Peter Diamond and Emmanuel Saez suggest that the optimal top tax rate for the U.S. is much closer to 75 percent than to 40 percent. There is considerable room to raise the top tax rates on ordinary income and capital gains.

Improving health outcomes through better access to health care could reduce the burden of rising income inequality and perhaps actually help to reduce it.

Macroeconomic Stabilization Policy. High unemployment rates mean the loss of labor income for a large number of workers. Replacement income—social insurance and public assistance benefits—often leads to a large reduction in living standards and movement toward the lower tail of the income distribution. Furthermore, a large proportion of the U.S. unemployed have been without work for over 6 months, which may leave permanent scars on the long-term unemployed that could prevent them from ever regaining their pre-unemployment living standards. High unemployment levels increase the lower tail of the income distribution and perhaps hollows out the middle of the distribution. Consequently, macroeconomic policies (both fiscal and monetary policies) to keep the unemployment rate low and to rapidly increase employment after recessions is critical to preventing a rise in inequality. After a brief flirtation with expansionary fiscal policy in 2008 and 2009, the U.S. essentially adopted an austerity program (mostly by default due to Congressional gridlock) and monetary policy alone has not been up to the task of rapidly reducing high unemployment levels. Consequently, the U.S. has about 2 million fewer jobs in mid-2013 than it did at the start of the Great Recession in December 2007.

Labor Market Policy. Two long-term shifts in the U.S. have kept wages low for many workers. The inflation-adjusted value of the minimum wage has fallen dramatically since the 1960s. At the same time, the private-sector unionization rate has fallen. While these shifts have benefited the Walton family and Walmart shareholders (those in the upper tail of the income distribution) they have harmed Walmart workers who are mostly in the lower tail of the income distribution. The national policies to counteract these shifts require some legislative action, which is unlikely to happen as long as the Republican Party retains control of the U.S. House of Representatives. Some actions, however, can be taken at the subnational level; for example, some states have a higher minimum wage than the federal minimum wage of $7.25 per hour.

Human Capital Investment. Increasing educational levels and improving the quality of education is one policy that almost all observers agree upon. This would reduce income inequality to the extent that skill-biased technological change is a source of rising income inequality. But this is not the only human capital investment that would affect inequality. Improving health outcomes through better access to health care could reduce the burden of rising income inequality and perhaps actually help to reduce it. Poor childhood health has been linked with low parental income and low socio-economic status. Poor childhood health also is related to reduced human capital accumulation and poor labor market outcomes (high unemployment and low wages) later in life. Early interventions to improve childhood health could lead to improved labor market outcomes in adulthood and upward income mobility. This would require better access to quality health care for lower income families, which is one of the goals of the recent U.S. health care legislation often referred to as "Obamacare."

Income inequality in the United States rose significantly over the past 50 years. Income has become more concentrated at the top of the income distribution but more people appear to have become concentrated at the bottom of the distribution. The social ills associated with inequality have made a large proportion of Americans worse off in terms of income, health, and political participation. Given what we know about the rise in income disparities, the policy remedies are not drastic. As a matter of fact, some of the policies, such as higher tax rates on high-income taxpayers and a higher minimum wage, were in place 50 years ago when economic growth was higher and income disparities were lower.

4

Income Inequality Is Not Unfair and Does Not Need to Be Eliminated

Arthur C. Brooks

Arthur C. Brooks is president of the American Enterprise Institute and author of The Battle: How the Fight Between Free Enterprise and Big Government Will Shape America's Future.

Most Americans believe in equality of opportunity but not equality of outcome. A minority pushing for equality of outcome has used the language of fairness to make income inequality seem like a problem to be remedied. In fact, people do not have the right to equal income and to impose such equality would actually result in a distinctly unfair society.

In America we stand for equality. But for the large majority of us, this means equality of opportunity, not equality of outcome.

A Difference in Worldview

If you are like most Americans, you believe we all should start at more or less the same place with more or less the same opportunities to succeed in life. But you also believe that, within reason, it's perfectly all right if we end up in different places.

If you are in the 70 percent majority, you believe that everyone should get a chance to succeed. Or everyone should fail on his or her own merits. If this leads to income inequality—above some acceptable floor—so be it.

The intellectual and political leaders of the 30 percent coalition disagree. They prefer a world in which we all end up in roughly the same economic place regardless of our abilities and efforts.

This fundamental difference in worldview leads to a major disagreement about the role of government. The majority believes government should protect the returns for hard work and merit. The 30 percent coalition effectively wants the government to penalize success. This is America's culture war in a nutshell.

A Misleading Definition of Fairness

The definition of fairness for those in the 30 percent coalition, fundamentally at odds with the worldview of the 70 percent majority, is a huge liability for them. They have concealed the central pillar of their ideology—income inequality—under a misleading definition of fairness.

Legal equality, political equality, religious equality— almost all Americans would agree that these values are vital to our nation. But equality of income? That's a fundamentally different kind of equality.

They say one thing but mean another. The 70 percent majority needs to expose this fact and reclaim the language of fairness for the free enterprise system.

The 30 percent coalition is clever when it comes to redistribution. It would have you believe that income inequality is equivalent to equality in other areas, such as law or politics or religion. And because America, the world's first modern democracy, was founded on the principle of equality, its rhetoric can seem highly compelling if you don't think too deeply about it.

Legal equality, political equality, religious equality—almost all Americans would agree that these values are vital to our nation. But equality of income? That's a fundamentally different kind of equality.

We can all agree that everyone has an equal right to a fair trial, but we certainly don't all agree that everyone has a right to receive a verdict of "innocent." Only the innocent people deserve that.

Likewise, without our political system, we believe everyone has the right to vote, but we don't believe everyone has the right to see his or her chosen candidate elected to office.

The Unfairness of Equality of Outcome

This is what makes the 30 percent coalition's reliance on the rhetoric of "fairness" so duplicitous. It implies that equality of outcome is a core American principle, when in fact what Americans believe in is equality of opportunity and the potential to earn success.

It is easy to be intimidated by the rhetoric of "fairness." Nobody wants to sound anti-poor. It is no surprise, therefore, that many in the 70 percent majority have chosen just to cede to the 30 percent coalition the fairness issue and content themselves with making the case for economic efficiency.

Proponents of free enterprise must not make this mistake. Fairness should not be a 30 percent trump card but rather its Achilles' heel. Equality of income is not fair. It is distinctly unfair.

If you work harder than a coworker but are paid the same, that is unfair. If you save your money but still retire with the same pension as your spendthrift neighbor, that is unfair. And if you stay in your house and make the mortgage payments even when its value drops but your neighbor walks away without recourse, that is unfair.

5

A House Divided

Thomas J. Sugrue

Thomas J. Sugrue is the David Boies Professor of History and Sociology at the University of Pennsylvania and author of Not Even Past: Barack Obama and the Burden of Race.

An anecdotal story about a white family and a black family in the Detroit area illustrates how the wealth divide is created and maintained. Since housing is one of the main sources of family wealth, the differences in access to owning real estate and the value of real estate that exist along racial lines affect lifelong wealth accumulation. The bursting of the housing bubble and the predatory loans leading up to the bust negatively impacted the wealth of minority families to a greater degree than white families.

In 1973, my parents sold their modest house on Detroit's West Side to Roosevelt Smith, a Vietnam War veteran and an assembly-line worker at Ford, and his wife, Virginia (not their real names). For the Smiths—African Americans and native Mississippians—the neighborhood was an appealing place to raise their two young children, and the price was within their means: $17,500. The neighborhood's three-bedroom colonials and Tudors, mostly built between the mid-1920s and the late '40s, were well maintained, the streets quiet and lined with stately trees. Nearby was a movie theater, a good grocery store, a local department store, and a decent shopping district. Like many first-time home buyers, the Smiths had every reason to expect that their house would be an appreciating investment.

For their part, my parents moved to a rapidly growing suburb that would soon be incorporated as Farmington Hills. Their new house, on a quiet, curvilinear street, was a significant step up from the Detroit place. It had four bedrooms, a two-car attached garage, and a large yard. It cost them $43,000. Within a few years, they had added a family room and expanded the small rear patio. Their subdivision, like most in Farmington Hills, was carefully zoned. The public schools were modern and well funded, with substantial revenues from the town's mostly middle- and upper-middle-class taxpayers. All of the creature comforts of the good suburban life were close at hand: shopping malls, swim clubs, movie theaters, good restaurants.

My parents lived in the Farmington house for a little over twenty years. When my father retired in the mid-1990s, the property had appreciated by about $100,000. They did not get rich from the proceeds of their home sale—indeed, after adjusting for inflation, the house was worth slightly less than they paid for it, not even counting interest costs and taxes. But it nonetheless allowed them to walk away with about $80,000.

Places like Farmington Hills, which were all white in the '70s and '80s, were direct beneficiaries of Detroit's decline.

For the Smiths it was a far different story. Detroit had been losing population since the 1950s, and especially after the 1967 riots there was massive "white flight" from the city. The neighborhood in which the Smiths invested went from mostly white to black within a few years, along with the rest of Detroit. For the city as a whole, those who remained were not as well off on average as those who left, meaning that even as the tax base shrank, the demand for city services went up, setting off a vicious death spiral. Soon, schools and infrastructure groaned with age, and the city's tax base shrank further as businesses relocated to suburban office parks and shopping centers. By the end of the '70s, the decline of the auto industry and manufacturing generally compounded Detroit's woes, as production shifted to Japan or the South in search of cheaper labor and fewer regulations.

As the downward cycle continued, investors and absentee landlords—fearful that their property values would decline as Detroit got poorer and blacker—let their properties run down. Rising crime led to a drop in pedestrian traffic both downtown and in neighborhood shopping districts, and also to increasing demand for additional police protection. As the cost of city services surged and the tax base shrank, Detroit came to have among the highest property tax rates in the nation, which was another reason for people to move out if they could.

Meanwhile, places like Farmington Hills, which were all white in the '70s and '80s, were direct beneficiaries of Detroit's decline. The seemingly insatiable demand for suburban real estate raised housing values; well-funded schools attracted families with children; local malls had few, if any, vacancies; and new shops and office parks seemed to spring up daily.

The same year that my father retired, I visited my childhood neighborhood, and drove past the Smiths' house. The lawn was lush, the shrubs well tended. They had built a garage. The old siding had been replaced and the original windows updated. I stopped at a local real estate broker's office to check out the housing prices in the area. The Smiths' home was not for sale, but another house just two blocks away, almost identical to it and in move-in condition, was on the market for $24,500. Over two decades, Roosevelt and Virginia

Smith's house in my parents' old neighborhood, despite love and care and investments, had appreciated by only about $7,000. After adjusting for inflation, their house was worth about 60 percent less than they had paid for it.

In the United States, where real estate is the single largest source of asset accumulation for the middle class, the story of the Sugrues and the Smiths goes a long way to explaining the expanding disparities between white and black wealth. The two families—like many Americans—invested in real estate both for its use value and as a gamble on the future. But one family did far, far better than the other.

The racial wealth gap has several specific causes beyond the broad legacy of systematic racial segregation, discrimination, and unequal opportunity.

Every once in a while, a scholarly book fundamentally shifts how we understand a problem. One of those books was published in 1995, two years after my parents sold their house. Sociologists Melvin Oliver and Thomas Shapiro's *Black Wealth/ White Wealth* stepped into a stale debate about race, class, and inequality in the United States with new data and a fresh perspective. The authors acknowledged the gains of the civil rights era: Black-white income gaps had narrowed. Minorities were better represented at elite institutions of higher education than could have been imagined in 1960. And while in the '60s the most prominent black elites were car dealers or owners of "race businesses" that catered to black customers, by the end of the twentieth century the number of black engineers, lawyers, and corporate executives had grown. Newsmagazines trumpeted the high incomes of black sports stars and celebrities. "The New Black Middle Class" became a tagline. African Americans might not have wholly overcome the legacy of centuries of slavery and segregation, but they had come a long way.

But Oliver and Shapiro told another story, a sobering one about the persistent gap between black and white wealth. They methodically gathered and analyzed data about household assets, like real estate holdings, bank accounts, stocks and bonds, cars, and other property, that constitute a family's portfolio. Their findings were staggering: despite all of the gains of the previous quarter century, the median black family had only 8 percent of the household wealth of the median white family. The asset gap was still strikingly wide among middle-class and wealthy blacks, who, despite their high incomes, still had about a third the assets of comparable whites.

The racial wealth gap has several specific causes beyond the broad legacy of systematic racial segregation, discrimination, and unequal opportunity. Wealth is passed down from generation to generation—even if only modestly. But going back generations, blacks had little opportunity to get a stake hold. Upon emancipation, they were mostly penniless, without land or access to credit, and almost all blacks were excluded from the various Homestead Acts that, beginning in 1862, allowed so many poor white families to accumulate land and, with it, wealth.

Meanwhile, most African Americans earned too little to save: most lacked access to the loans and capital necessary to start a business or buy stock or own their own homes. Lack of financial assets made African Americans more vulnerable to unemployment and medical emergencies, less likely to be able to pay for their children's college education, and more likely to be stuck with the burden of supporting impoverished parents or to face poverty themselves in old age.

Even with the coming of Social Security and stronger protections for organized labor under the New Deal, most blacks were excluded from the benefits because they worked as tenant farmers or domestics who were not covered by the new plans. Two other Depression-era federal programs—the Home Owners' Loan Corporation and the Federal Housing Administration—encouraged homeownership and bankrolled suburbanization, but in the North and South alike, whole neighborhoods were redlined, many of them black.

A recent study of data from the Home Mortgage Disclosure Act found that 32.1 percent of wealthy blacks, but only 10.5 percent of wealthy whites, got higher-priced mortgages.

Many African Americans lost out on the benefits of the post-World War II GI Bill as well. As Ira Katznelson points out in his book *When Affirmative Action Was White*, of the 3,229 home, business, and farm loans made under the GI Bill in Mississippi during 1947, black veterans received only two. Until 1968, it was virtually impossible for blacks to get access to the kinds of long-term, low-interest mortgages that made wide-scale homeownership possible.

Even after the passage of civil rights laws, dozens of studies showed that minorities had a harder time getting access to market-rate mortgages. Moreover, black home buyers were likely to be steered to neighborhoods of older housing stock, often in declining central cities, places where housing values often depreciated rather than appreciated. This meant that blacks, if they were lucky enough to be homeowners, were often trapped in neighborhoods on the margins, economically and politically. As it turns out, the Sugrues and the Smiths were fairly typical of the black and white families that Oliver and Shapiro studied in the mid-'90s. And what has happened since then is even more disheartening.

Beginning in the '90s and lasting until the bursting of the real estate bubble, some progress was made. The percentage of black households that owned their own homes increased from 43.3 percent in 1994 to 47.2 percent in 2007. Partly this reflected a still-growing black middle class; partly it reflected important government efforts to end racial discrimination in mortgage lending, along with the arrival of new, responsibly crafted forms of mortgages for which more people, particularly African Americans and Latinos, could qualify.

But around the turn of the twenty-first century, there also grew up a huge new industry of predatory lenders that targeted members of minority groups, including those who already owned their homes and were persuaded to refinance on what turned out to be usurious terms. In 2006, more than half of the loans made to African Americans were subprime, compared to about a quarter for whites. And a recent study of data from the Home Mortgage Disclosure Act found that 32.1 percent of wealthy blacks, but only 10.5 percent of wealthy whites, got higher-priced mortgages—those with an interest rate 3 or more points higher than the rate of a Treasury security of the same length.

The Brandeis Institute on Assets and Social Policy estimates that only 8 percent of black seniors and only 4 percent of Latino seniors have sufficient economic resources to be economically secure in retirement.

The bursting of the real estate bubble has been a catastrophe for the broad American middle class as a whole, but it has been particularly devastating to African Americans. According to the Center for Responsible Lending in Durham, North Carolina, nearly 25 percent of African Americans who bought or refinanced their homes between 2004 and 2008 (and an equivalent share among Latinos) have already lost or will end up losing their homes—compared to 11.9 percent of white families in the same situation. This disparate impact of the housing crash has made the racial gap in wealth even more extreme. As Reid Cramer, director of the Asset Building Program at the New America Foundation, puts it, "Basically, we have gone from an average minority family owning 10 cents to the dollar compared to the average white family to now owning less than a nickel." The median black family today holds only $4,955 in assets.

In recent years, concerns about racial disparities have largely faded from national politics. It is now a commonplace that we have entered a post-racial era. The concerns of the civil rights era are obsolete. A black family occupies the White House. Conservative jurists and even many liberals are arguing with greater conviction than ever that affirmative action programs and the Voting Rights Act are no longer necessary in a color-blind America. For his part, the first African American president has been remarkably silent on questions of race. University of Pennsylvania political scientist Daniel Gillion examined decades of presidential speeches and found that Barack Obama has said less about race than any Democratic president since 1961.

But for all of the talk about hope and change, the racial wealth gap has not only persisted, it has worsened. And it is this gap that is the most powerful measure of differential well-being by race. Wealth has profound consequences throughout the life cycle, from putting a down payment on a first home to spending your last days in a skilled nursing facility. Starting a business? Paying for college tuition? Making ends meet when you've lost your job? Covering extraordinary medical expenses? Retiring? Assets matter.

On each of these counts, minorities face an insecure present and a very precarious future. Consider just one measure: the Brandeis Institute on Assets and Social Policy estimates that only 8 percent of black seniors and only 4 percent of Latino seniors have sufficient economic resources to be economically secure in retirement. "These seniors," write a team of Brandeis scholars, "do not just have to watch their pennies; they are truly struggling every day, forgoing basic expenditures, such as medical appointments and household maintenance, just to make ends meet."

A few years ago, I met Roosevelt Smith. He still owned my parents' old house on Detroit's West Side, which was a rental property by then, and he gave me a tour. It was in good shape—pretty much the same house that my parents sold, but with newly refinished floors and some new kitchen cabinets and tiles and the garage out back. He's a resourceful guy who bought a second, larger house nearby—another asset, a nest egg for the future. But together, the two houses aren't worth much. The median listing price for homes in Detroit is now just $21,000, or about the cost of a Chevy Malibu—and, like the car, likely to depreciate in value from the moment you buy it. Detroit's population has fallen from 1.85 million in 1950 to a little more than 700,000 today, and as population falls housing demand falls with it. Today, nearly every block has abandoned homes on it. The Smiths probably have more in household assets than the $4,955 median for black families, but not a lot.

In contrast, my parents' assets have provided them with a cushion of security and more than modest comfort, from that family room they built in the '70s to the cottage in northern Michigan they built forty years ago and later renovated for their retirement. Along the way, my parents used their savings to help pay for three college tuitions. They helped me buy my first house because I didn't have enough savings for the 10 percent down payment. When their health deteriorated, they drew from their assets to rent an apartment in a comfortable retirement community. Barring a medical disaster, which my mother could at least partially cover using her remaining assets, my sisters and I can expect a small sum from her estate. Last year, my mother sent me a check—she called it, rather morbidly, a "down payment" on my inheritances—that totaled more than twice the household assets of the median black family.

I have never thought of myself as a particularly wealthy person, and by the standards of the top 1 percent I'm not one.

Despite the swings of the economy and a divorce settlement that drained my retirement account, I own a house worth more than twice its original purchase price. I have squirreled away some money in a mutual fund to help pay for my children's educational expenses: college is just a few years off, and it won't be cheap. I can also use some of my assets as collateral for loans to help pay their way. And, if my investment decisions prove to be wise, I will have a substantially larger retirement nest egg than my parents had. If I have extraordinary medical expenses, I have funds to fall back on. I also drafted a will, and hope that my heirs—my family and a few charities—will be able to benefit from my good fortune.

There are many white folks who are not as fortunate as my parents were, and even the modest legacy they were able to build may be becoming increasingly rare among younger generations of Americans of all races. Still, like most whites, I am a beneficiary of the racial wealth gap. And until that gap narrows, we can't begin to talk about the dawning of a post-racial America.

6

Disparities in Achievement Along Racial and Ethnic Lines Are the Norm

Thomas Sowell

Thomas Sowell is the Rose and Milton Friedman Senior Fellow at the Hoover Institution at Stanford University.

Disparities in income are often created by disparities in abilities. Disparities in special skills and achievements along racial and ethnic lines are common throughout the world. Yet, when disparities in employment and income materialize, critics often assume that such disparities are the result of discrimination, rather than natural talent. It is improper to blame those who are members of groups that achieve success for the failures of other groups.

With all the talk about "disparities" in innumerable contexts, there is one very important disparity that gets remarkably little attention—disparities in the ability to create wealth. People who are preoccupied, or even obsessed, with disparities in income are seldom interested much, or at all, in the disparities in the ability to create wealth, which are often the reasons for the disparities in income.

The Inequality of Ability

In a market economy, people pay us for benefiting them in some way—whether we are sweeping their floors, selling them diamonds or anything in between. Disparities in our ability to

Thomas Sowell, "An Ignored 'Disparity,'" *Townhall*, January 17, 2012. Copyright © 2012 Townhall. All rights reserved. By permission of Thomas Sowell and Creators Syndicate, Inc.

create benefits for which others will pay us are huge, and the skills required can develop early—or sometimes not at all.

A recent national competition among high school students who create their own technological advances turned up an especially high share of such students winning recognition in the San Francisco Bay Area. A closer look showed that the great majority of these Bay Area students had Asian names.

Asian Americans are a substantial presence in this region but they are by no means a majority, much less such an overwhelming majority as they are among those winning high tech awards.

This pattern of disproportionate representation of particular groups among those with special skills and achievements is not confined to Asian Americans or even to the United States.

It is a phenomenon among particular racial, ethnic or other groups in countries around the worlds—the Ibos in Nigeria, the Parsees in India, the Armenians in the Ottoman Empire, Germans in Brazil, Chinese in Malaysia, Lebanese in West Africa, Tamils in Sri Lanka. The list goes on and on.

Nowhere have [human] achievements been random or representative of the demographic proportions of the population of a country or of the world.

The Assumption About Racial and Ethnic Differences

Gross inequalities in skills and achievements have been the rule, not the exception, on every inhabited continent and for centuries on end. Yet our laws and government policies act as if any significant statistical difference between racial or ethnic groups in employment or income can only be a result of their being treated differently by others.

Nor is this simply an opinion. Businesses have been sued by the government when the representation of different groups among their employees differs substantially from their proportions in the population at large. But, no matter how the human race is broken down into its components—whether by race, sex, geographic region or whatever—glaring disparities in achievements have been the rule, not the exception.

Anyone who watches professional basketball games knows that the star players are by no means a representative sample of the population at large. The book *Human Accomplishment* by Charles Murray is a huge compendium of the top achievements around the world in the arts and sciences, as well as in sports and other fields.

Nowhere have these achievements been random or representative of the demographic proportions of the population of a country or of the world. Nor have they been the same from one century to the next. China was once far more advanced technologically than any country in Europe, but then it fell behind and more recently is gaining ground.

Blaming Failure on the Success of Others

Most professional golfers who participate in PGA tournaments have never won a single tournament, but Arnold Palmer, Jack Nicklaus and Tiger Woods have each won dozens of tournaments.

Yet these and numerous other disparities in achievement are resolutely ignored by those whose shrill voices denounce disparities in rewards, as if these disparities are somehow suspicious at best and sinister at worst.

Higher achieving groups—whether classes, races or whatever—are often blamed for the failure of other groups to achieve. Politicians and intellectuals, especially, tend to conceive of social questions in terms that allow them to take on the role of being on the side of the angels against the forces of evil.

This can be a huge disservice to those individuals and groups who are lagging behind, for it leads them to focus on a sense of grievance and victimhood, rather than on how they can lift themselves up instead of trying to pull other people down.

Again, this is a worldwide phenomenon—a sad commentary on the down side of the brotherhood of man.

7

Race, Wealth, and Intergenerational Poverty

Darrick Hamilton

Darrick Hamilton is an associate professor of economics and urban policy at The New School, an affiliate scholar of the Center for American Progress, and a research affiliate at the Research Network on Racial and Ethnic Inequality at Duke University.

The persistent wealth gap between whites and blacks in the United States is the most prominent sign of racial inequality and proves that American society has not risen above the racial divide. The explanations given for racial differences in behavior are not supported by research. Blacks have fewer resources than whites partly owing to the history of slavery and the barriers to owning land after the Civil War. Government intervention is necessary to correct the wrongs of the past and eventually eliminate the racial wealth divide.

Despite an enormous and persistent black-white wealth gap, the ascendant American narrative is one that proclaims our society has transcended the racial divide. But wealth is a paramount indicator of social well-being. Wealthier families are better positioned to afford elite education, access capital to start a business, finance expensive medical procedures, reside in higher amenity neighborhoods, exert political influence through campaign contributions, purchase better legal representation, leave a bequest, and withstand financial hardship resulting from an emergency.

The wealth gap is the most acute indicator of racial inequality. Based on data from the 2002 Survey of Income and Program Participation, white median household net worth is about $90,000; in contrast it is only about $8,000 for the median Latino household and a mere $6,000 for the median black household. The median Latino or black household would have to save nearly 100 percent of its income for at least three consecutive years to close the gap. Furthermore, 85 percent of black and Latino households have a net worth below the median white household. Regardless of age, household structure, education, occupation, or income, black households typically have less than a quarter of the wealth of otherwise comparable white households.

Since the election of Barack Obama, a growing belief has emerged that race is no longer a defining feature of one's life chances. But the extraordinary overlap between wealth and race puts a lie to the notion that America is now in a post-racial era. The smallest racial wealth gap exists for families in the third quartile of the income distribution where the typical black family has only 38 percent of the wealth of the typical white family. In the bottom income quartile—the group containing the working poor—a black family has a startingly low 2 percent of the wealth of the typical white family.

Those who recognize the racial wealth gap but still embrace the idea of a post-racial America have crafted two explanations for this disparity. The first is that, in search of immediate gratification, blacks are less frugal when it comes to savings. Indeed, in an April lecture at Morehouse College, Federal Reserve Chair Ben Bernanke attributed the racial wealth gap to a lack of "financial" literacy on the part of blacks, particularly with respect to savings behavior.

Such an explanation, however, is not the case. Economists ranging from Milton Friedman to Marjorie Galenson to the recently deceased founder of the Caucus of Black Economists, Marcus Alexis, found that, after accounting for household income, blacks historically have had a slightly higher savings rate than whites. In 2004, economists Maury Gittleman and Edward Wolff also found that blacks save at a moderately higher rate than do whites, again after adjusting for household income. This indicates even greater black frugality because many higher-income blacks offer more support to lower-income relatives than do whites, further reducing their resources to save.

During the 1999–2001 recession, median household wealth fell by 27 percent for both Latinos and blacks, while it grew by 2 percent for whites.

The second explanation given to support the post-racial narrative is that inferior management of assets owned by blacks has resulted in lower portfolio returns. However, recent research finds no significant racial differences in asset appreciation rates for families with positive net worth.

Recessions disproportionately affect black and Latino families. During the 1999–2001 recession, median household wealth fell by 27 percent for both Latinos and blacks, while it grew by 2 percent for whites. The current recession likely will worsen the racial wealth gap. Although whites are more likely than blacks to own their home, the share of black wealth in the form of housing is nearly twice as large as the white share. And with blacks far more likely than whites to have been steered toward sub-prime loans in discriminatory credit markets, the foreclosure crisis is bound to have a more deleterious effect on black wealth than on white wealth.

For example, a recent report on mortgage lending and race by the Institute on Race and Poverty at the University of

Minnesota found that black Twin City residents earning over $150,000, in comparison to whites earning below $40,000, were twice as likely to be denied a home loan. Those fortunate (or unfortunate) enough to get a loan were more than three times as likely to have a sub-prime loan.

Economic studies also demonstrate that inheritances, bequests, and intra-family transfers account for more of the racial wealth gap than any other demographic and socioeconomic factor, including education, income, and household structure. These intra-familial transfers, the primary source of wealth for most Americans with positive net worth, are transfers of blatant non-merit resources. Why do blacks have vastly fewer resources to leave to the next generation?

Apart from the national failure to endow ex-slaves with the promised 40 acres and a mule after the Civil War, blacks were deprived systematically of property, especially land, accumulated between 1880 and 1910 by government complicity and fraud as well as seizures by white terrorists. During the first three decades of the 20th century, white rioters destroyed prosperous black communities from Wilmington, North Carolina, to Tulsa, Oklahoma. Restrictive covenants, redlining, and general housing and lending discrimination also inhibited blacks from accumulating wealth.

Wealth . . . can be an effective non-race-based instrument to eliminate racial inequality.

Given the importance of intergenerational transfers of wealth and past and present barriers preventing black wealth accumulation, private action and market forces alone cannot close an unjust racial wealth gap—public-sector intervention is necessary.

Indeed, the public sector already subsidizes asset acquisition. A 2004 report by the Corporation for Enterprise Development estimates that, even before the current financial crisis, the federal government allocated $335 billion of its 2003 budget in the form of tax subsidies and savings to promote asset development such as mortgage deductions. This excluded any corporate subsidies and tax savings and was more than 15 times the amount spent on education.

At issue is not the amount but the recipients. Those earning over $1 million a year received about one third of the entire allocation, while the bottom 60 percent of earners received only 5 percent. Individuals in the bottom 20 percent typically received a measly $4.24 benefit. A more progressive distribution could be transformative for low-income Americans.

The surge in the post-racial perspective has moved us away from race-specific policies. However, wealth, given the racial disparity of its distribution, can be an effective non-race-based instrument to eliminate racial inequality. We could shift from an income-based to a wealth-based test for transfer programs. Policy eligibility based on net worth below the national median would qualify a large proportion of black households. Electronic financial records and publicly available home appraisals now make it easier to estimate net worth, and to avoid savings crowd-out, the program could be structured similarly to the Earned Income Tax Credit program, which uses a phase-out schedule to avoid work disincentives.

These changes in eligibility should be coupled with policies to promote asset building. For example, the American Dream Demonstration program uses individual development accounts to create match incentives for low-income savers. Another initiative, the Saving for Education, Entrepreurship, and Downpayment, established children's development accounts (sometimes called "baby bonds") to create endowed trusts for children at birth. In the United Kingdom, since 2005, every newborn receives a trust ranging from 250 pounds to 500 pounds depending on familial resources.

In 2004, the American Saving for Personal Investment, Retirement, and Education (ASPIRE) Act was introduced in Congress to establish children's development accounts in the U.S. While the nation's first black president eschews race-specific policies, perhaps a strongly amended ASPIRE bill designed to progressively distribute funds based on familial net worth can be the policy that enables him to "bind . . . [black America's] grievances . . . to the larger aspirations of all Americans."

We envision a "baby bond" plan of much greater magnitude—progressively rising to $50,000 or $60,000 for children in families in the lowest wealth quartile and accessible once the child turns 18 years of age. We also would determine eligibility for such a program based upon the net-worth position, rather than the income, of the child's family (all children whose family fell below the national median for wealth would receive baby bonds).

We should strive not for a race-neutral America but a race-fair America. For that to occur, the transmission of racial economic advantage or disadvantage across generations would have to cease. Public provision of a substantial trust fund for newborns from wealth-poor families would also go a long way toward achieving the ideal.

8

How to Fix America's Wealth Inequality: Teach Americans to Be Cheap

Noah Smith

Noah Smith is an assistant professor of finance at Stony Brook University in New York State.

There is wealth inequality in the United States and there are reasons why government should do more to increase the wealth of the poor. Wealth redistribution is one mechanism for decreasing the wealth divide, and income redistribution can help fix the problem. But the best way to address wealth inequality is to provide basic financial education in schools and encourage people to be more frugal and save more.

There's a video making the rounds, showing America's staggering wealth inequality. As the sheer magnitude of the disparity unfolds behind the narrator's calm, steady voice, one struggles not to feel a sense of creeping horror. Did you know that the richest 1% of Americans owned 40% of the country's total wealth? I actually didn't!

Now, a word of caution: A lot of that wealth inequality is actually age, not class. Young people tend to have a lot of debt and not much savings, meaning they have negative wealth (a prime example being yours truly). Also, these statistics don't include things like entitlements, or human capital (the value of your skills and education). So Americans aren't quite as unequal as the video makes out. But they are still very, very unequal.

So what should we do about this? First, we need to ask ourselves if we should do anything about wealth inequality. At first it seems obvious, but consider this: Usually, what we care about is not the wealth of the poor and the middle class, but how much they get to consume. Those aren't the same thing. In the short run, in fact, they're the opposite—every dollar you save (which goes straight to your "wealth") is a dollar you don't spend on food, or clothes, or gas, or housing, or something else you can actually use.

So maybe we should just worry about consumption equality, and let the rich sit on their useless stock portfolios like Smaug the dragon sitting on his giant pile of gold.

Or maybe not. First of all, living hand-to-mouth is no way to live. Wealth gives people a security cushion, meaning they don't have to borrow money if they get sick or lose their job. Security translates to peace of mind. Also, wealth affects political power; a more unequal wealth distribution means that government will be captured by a narrower range of interests. But most importantly, though there is a wealth/consumption trade-off in the short run, in the long run there is quite the opposite; the rich, it turns out, make a hefty chunk of their income from the returns that accrue to their wealth.

The Origin of Wealth Inequality

The math of wealth is actually pretty simple: It all boils down to four things: 1. How much you start with, 2. How much income you make, 3. How much of your income you save, and 4. How good of a rate of return you get on your savings.

So one obvious thing we could do to make wealth more equal is—surprise!—redistribution. It turns out that *income* redistribution and *wealth* redistribution have much the same effect on the wealth of the poor and middle-class. Income redistribution is probably a bit better, for two reasons. First, people with higher incomes tend to save more, meaning they build wealth more rapidly. Second, people with higher incomes tend to have less risk aversion, meaning they are more willing to invest in assets like stocks (which get high average rates of return, although they are risky) rather than safe assets like savings accounts and CDs that get low rates of return.

The most potent way to get more wealth to the poor and middle-class is to get these people to save more of their income, and to invest in assets with higher average rates of return.

In other words, giving the poor and middle-class more income will boost the amount they are *able* to save, the percentage they are *willing* to save, and the *return* they get on those savings. Part of the reason America's wealth distribution is so unequal in the first place is that our income distribution is very unequal.

But there are reasons to believe that redistribution can't fix all of the problem, or even most of it. If you do the math, you discover that in the long run, income levels and initial wealth (factors 1 and 2 from above) are not the main determinants of wealth. They are dwarfed by factors 3 and 4—savings rates and rates of return. The most potent way to get more wealth to the poor and middle-class is to get these people to save more of their income, and to invest in assets with higher average rates of return.

As I mentioned, income redistribution helps these things a bit, but it doesn't account for the whole difference. The rich probably save more than the poor for many more reasons besides the simple fact that they're rich. In fact, being willing to save more is probably a big part of how the rich got rich in the first place. "Cheap" is an insult, but being cheap is how you get rich. If you consume everything you earn, your consumption will be higher today, but lower twenty years down the road; in our consumption-focused society, a lot of people are caught in this trap. And government can and should help them get out.

Saving the Poor Through Savings

What can government do to get middle-class and poor people to save more? Higher interest rates don't do the trick—people didn't save more in the early 80s when interest rates were stratospheric. High stock returns don't do the trick either—in the booming 1990s, people actually saved less, seeming to prefer to "let the market do their saving for them."

Instead, the answer is to change America's culture of (not) saving. This sounds hard, but actually it is probably very doable. For years, behavioral economists such as Richard Thaler have been studying ways to "nudge" people to save more. The most famous "nudge," which has been endorsed by President Obama, is to make employee pension plans "opt-out" instead of "opt-in". But there are plenty of others. In lab experiments, just giving people information on how to save money makes them save a lot more.

In the long run, "asset allocation"—i.e., how much of your savings you put in stocks and other high-return assets like corporate bonds—is a major determinant of whose wealth grows and whose stays the same.

This means that more financial education in public schools is a must. I'm not talking about teaching kids the Capital Asset Pricing Model. I mean what Bob Shiller calls "basic Suze Orman stuff." How to make a monthly budget. What "saving" and "borrowing" mean. How wealth builds over time. How to avoid borrowing lots of money at high interest rates (e.g. credit cards and payday loans). Etc. The new Consumer Financial Protection Bureau can help a lot with this too, by preventing companies from tricking poor people into taking out high-interest debt.

Return to Equality

In addition to "nudging" middle-class and poor Americans to save more, we can help them get a better return on their assets—the second thing that has a huge effect on wealth in the long run. This means helping middle-class people invest in stocks without paying high fees. The first part of this is teaching middle-class people to avoid making frequent changes in their stock portfolios. Studies show that individual investors consistently lose money when they try to buy and sell and buy and sell, mostly because they tend to ignore *trading* costs. So financial education should teach people to let their stock portfolios just sit there for decades, and ignore the ups and downs.

The second way to get better returns is to avoid actively managed funds. Actively managed mutual funds charge high fees to purchase portfolios of stocks that, statistically, are no better than simply buying a low-cost "index" fund that tracks the overall level of the market. Pension plans like TIAA-CREF tend to charge even higher fees, meaning even worse returns. Financial education can teach middle-class people what a low-cost index fund is, and how to invest in one.

This is not to say that middle-class people should put all their money in stocks. And many poor people can't afford to take the risk of investing in stocks. But in the long run, "asset allocation"—i.e., how much of your savings you put in stocks and other high-return assets like corporate bonds—is a major determinant of whose wealth grows and whose stays the same. The government, through financial education and "nudge" programs, can help people take advantage of high-return investment opportunities without paying high fees and trading costs.

In the short run, wealth equality is closely tied to income equality. But in the long run, it's all about thrift, frugality, and saving—in other words, cheapness. If America's middle-class and poor people learn to be more cheap, then in 30 years, we will see a very different distribution of wealth.

9

Reflections on Inequality

Robert A. Levy

Robert A. Levy is chairman of the board of directors at the Cato Institute.

There is an unequal distribution of wealth in the United States. A growing economy tends to increase income inequality, but the wealthy lose much more during recessions. The wealthy already pay a large share of taxes, yet advocates for income equality call for more. People who gain their wealth through industriousness should not have to give their money to people who are idle. In fact, it would be immoral to demand that a wealthy person do so against his or her will.

Israeli president Shimon Peres reminds us: "By and large, those in the world who placed freedom above equality have done better by equality than those who placed equality above freedom have done by freedom." That observation, apparently lost on the Occupy Wall Street crowd, has a moral component as well: It is more just to reward effort, even if it cannot be proven to benefit the least affluent, than it is to reward the least affluent, even if they exert little effort to improve their status. Moral superiority does not entail punishing the industrious wealthy to sustain the indolent poor.

The Unequal Distribution of Wealth

Yet some people are economically deprived due to circumstances beyond their control. Even Ayn Rand, a radical laissez-faire capitalist, condones "helping other people, if and when they are worthy of the help and you can afford to help them." But Rand would certainly not interpose the state to coerce more equal distributions of wealth. It may be morally right to help the poor; but in a completely free society we would have a political right not to do so—even if sometimes, the exercise of that right might be considered heartless. Put differently, a theory of justice is not always congruent with a theory of politics. One can condemn ignoble conduct—lying, infidelity, and so on—without empowering government to take remedial action. "Governments are instituted among men," wrote Jefferson in the Declaration, to secure "certain unalienable Rights" including "the Pursuit of Happiness." Notably, it is the right to pursue, not necessarily attain, happiness that the social contract secures.

Fans of Occupy Wall Street fail to distinguish between two strikingly different groups of upper-income individuals: first, persons producing wealth by supplying goods and services that satisfy market needs; second, crony capitalists seeking bounty from D.C. bureaucrats.

Advocates for greater income equality cite statistics purporting to show growing disparities. Disingenuously, the data end in 2007, although 2009 information is available. Internal Revenue reports that total income of individuals in the top 1 percent fell more than 30 percent from 2007 to 2009. During that same period, income of the bottom 90 percent fell less than 3 percent. Here's the paradox: Equality improves during recessions because the wealthy, who take more risks and rely heavily on investments, lose the most. Understandably, no one promotes economic decline to redress inequality. Earnings gaps will tend to grow as the economy grows. Moreover, the Organization for Economic Cooperation and Development reports that inequality has grown faster over the past 30 years in Sweden, Germany, Israel, Finland, and New Zealand than here, despite their liberal welfare systems. Besides, wealth in the United States is relatively mobile. A November 2011 Federal Reserve study found that one-third of the richest 1 percent in 2007 were no longer in the richest 1 percent in 2009.

Further, the top 1 percent of income earners—persons earning more than $343,000 in 2009—paid 38 percent of income taxes. And that doesn't reflect the nondeductibility of capital losses, the tax on illusory gains due to inflation, and the double tax paid indirectly by shareholders on corporate profits before they're distributed or impounded in stock prices. By contrast, according to the Committee on Joint Taxation, more than half of American households paid zero income taxes. Those numbers are astonishing. Even persons who embrace progressive taxation are hard-pressed to argue that the tax code is insufficiently discriminatory. How far must progressivity extend to satisfy the left's notion of fairness?

The Reality of Inequalities

Yes, payroll taxes are regressive; although Social Security, in theory, was supposed to dispense benefits in rough relationship to contributions. That hasn't happened—mostly because poor and minority workers have shorter life expectancies. Ironically, resistance from the left has foreclosed inheritable private accounts, which would have neutralized the life expectancy problem.

Perhaps most important, fans of Occupy Wall Street fail to distinguish between two strikingly different groups of upper-income individuals: first, persons producing wealth by supplying goods and services that satisfy market needs; second, crony capitalists seeking bounty from D.C. bureaucrats, who bestow their largesse on the politically influential.

Finally, not all inequalities are reflected in monetary outcomes. Some rich people are sickly, short, fat, and stupid. Some poor people are athletic, glamorous, and intelligent. Yet Occupy Wall Street's proposals for distributive justices are based solely on income or wealth. Paraphrasing Bill Niskanen, Cato's former chairman: One young man is healthy and handsome, spends his days on the beach, and chooses to earn minimum wage by busing tables at night. Another young man is confined to a wheelchair. Distracted by few of life's other pleasures, he makes $500,000 a year in various entrepreneurial activities. Who should redistribute what to whom? Indeed, which of the two men is creating jobs for an unemployed nation? And which of the two is being greedy—in the worst sense of that tainted word—by demanding something to which he has no moral or legal claim?

10

To Reduce Inequality, We Should Help the Poor Not Tax the Rich

James Q. Wilson

Prior to his death in 2012, James Q. Wilson was the Shattuck Professor of Government at Harvard University, the James Collins Professor of Management and Public Policy in the Anderson School of Management at University of California, Los Angeles, and the Ronald Reagan Professor of Public Policy at Pepperdine University's School of Public Policy.

Income inequality in the United States is significant, but most Americans find inequality to be an acceptable part of the American economic system. Factors that enhance wealth include education and working spouses; the poor frequently have low education or are unwed mothers. Thus, it is possible to increase education and marriage to help keep people from poverty, an option that is preferable to blaming the rich for wealth inequality.

There is no doubt that incomes are unequal in the United States—far more so than in most European nations. This fact is part of the impulse behind the Occupy Wall Street movement, whose members claim to represent the 99 percent of us against the wealthiest 1 percent. It has also sparked a major debate in the [2012] Republican presidential race, where former Massachusetts governor Mitt Romney has come under fire for his tax rates and his career as the head of a private-equity firm.

Questions About Inequality

And economic disparity was the recurring theme of President [Barack] Obama's State of the Union address on Tuesday [January 24, 2012]. "We can either settle for a country where a shrinking number of people do really well, while a growing number of Americans barely get by," the president warned, "or we can restore an economy where everyone gets a fair shot and everyone does their fair share."

But the mere existence of income inequality tells us little about what, if anything, should be done about it. First, we must answer some key questions. Who constitutes the prosperous and the poor? Why has inequality increased? Does an unequal income distribution deny poor people the chance to buy what they want? And perhaps most important: How do Americans feel about inequality?

To answer these questions, it is not enough to take a snapshot of our incomes; we must instead have a motion picture of them and of how people move in and out of various income groups over time.

We could reduce income inequality by trying to curtail the financial returns of education and the number of women in the workforce—but who would want to do that?

The Rich in America

The "rich" in America are not a monolithic, unchanging class. A study by Thomas A. Garrett, economist at the Federal Reserve Bank of St. Louis, found that less than half of people in the top 1 percent in 1996 were still there in 2005. Such mobility is hardly surprising: A business school student, for instance, may have little money and high debts, but nine years later he or she could be earning a big Wall Street salary and bonus.

Mobility is not limited to the top-earning households. A study by economists at the Federal Reserve Bank of Minneapolis found that nearly half of the families in the lowest fifth of income earners in 2001 had moved up within six years. Over the same period, more than a third of those in the highest fifth of income-earners had moved down. Certainly, there are people such as Warren Buffett and Bill Gates who are ensconced in the top tier, but far more common are people who are rich for short periods.

And who are the rich? Affluent people, compared with poor ones, tend to have greater education and spouses who work full time. The past three decades have seen significant increases in real earnings for people with advanced degrees. The Bureau of Labor Statistics found that between 1979 and 2010, hourly wages for men and women with at least a college degree rose by 33 percent and 20 percent, respectively, while they fell for all people with less than a high school diploma—by 9 percent for women and 31 percent for men.

Also, households with two earners have seen their incomes rise. This trend is driven in part by women's increasing workforce participation, which doubled from 1950 to 2005 and which began to place women in well-paid jobs by the early 1980s.

We could reduce income inequality by trying to curtail the financial returns of education and the number of women in the workforce—but who would want to do that?

The Poor in America

The real income problem in this country is not a question of who is rich, but rather of who is poor. Among the bottom fifth of income earners, many people, especially men, stay there their whole lives. Low education and unwed motherhood only exacerbate poverty, which is particularly acute among racial minorities. Brookings Institution economist Scott Winship has argued that two-thirds of black children in

America experience a level of poverty that only 6 percent of white children will ever see, calling it a "national tragedy."

Making the poor more economically mobile has nothing to do with taxing the rich and everything to do with finding and implementing ways to encourage parental marriage, teach the poor marketable skills and induce them to join the legitimate workforce. It is easy to suppose that raising taxes on the rich would provide more money to help the poor. But the problem facing the poor is not too little money, but too few skills and opportunities to advance themselves.

Income inequality has increased in this country and in practically every European nation in recent decades. The best measure of that change is the Gini index, named after the Italian statistician Corrado Gini, who designed it in 1912. The index values vary between zero, when everyone has exactly the same income, and 1, when one person has all of the income and everybody else has none. In mid-1970s America, the index was 0.316, but it had reached 0.378 by the late 2000s. One of the few nations to see its Gini value fall was Greece, which went from 0.413 in the 1970s to 0.307 in the late 2000s. So Greece seems to be reducing income inequality—but with little to buy, riots in the streets and economic opportunity largely limited to those partaking in corruption, the nation is hardly a model for anyone's economy.

Income as measured by the federal government is not a reliable indicator of well-being, but consumption is.

Poverty in America is certainly a serious problem, but the plight of the poor has been moderated by advances in the economy. Between 1970 and 2010, the net worth of American households more than doubled, as did the number of television sets and air-conditioning units per home. In his book *The Poverty of the Poverty Rate*, Nicholas Eberstadt shows that over the past 30 or so years, the percentage of low income children in the United States who are underweight has gone down, the share of low-income households lacking complete plumbing facilities has declined, and the area of their homes adequately heated has gone up. The fraction of poor households with a telephone, a television set and a clothes dryer has risen sharply.

In other words, the country has become more prosperous, as measured not by income but by consumption: In constant dollars, consumption by people in the lowest quintile rose by more than 40 percent over the past four decades.

Income as measured by the federal government is not a reliable indicator of well-being, but consumption is. Though poverty is a problem, it has become less of one.

American Views About Inequality

Historically, Americans have had an unusual attitude toward income inequality. In 1985, political scientists Sidney Verba and Gary Orren published a book that compared how liberals in Sweden and in the United States viewed such inequality. By four or five to one, the Swedish liberals were more likely than the American ones to believe that it was important to give workers equal pay. The Swedes were three times more likely than the Americans to favor putting a top limit on incomes. (The Swedes get a lot of what they want: Their Gini index is 0.259, much lower than America's.)

Sweden has maintained a low Gini index in part by having more progressive tax rates. If Americans wanted to follow the Swedish example, they could. But what is the morally fair way to determine tax rates—other than taxing everyone at the same rate? The case for progressive tax rates is far from settled; just read Kip Hagopian's recent essay in *Policy Review*, which makes a powerful argument against progressive taxation because it fails to take into account aptitude and work effort.

American views about inequality have not changed much in the past quarter-century. In their 2009 book *Class War?*

What Americans Really Think About Economic Inequality, political scientists Benjamin Page and Lawrence Jacobs report that big majorities, including poor people, agree that "it is 'still possible' to start out poor in this country, work hard, and become rich," and reject the view that it is the government's job to narrow the income gap. More recently, a December Gallup poll showed that 52 percent of Americans say inequality is "an acceptable part" of the nation's economic system, compared with 45 percent who deemed it a "problem that needs to be fixed." Similarly, 82 percent said economic growth is "extremely important" or "very important," compared with 46 percent saying that reducing the gap between rich and poor is extremely or very important.

A Strategy for Reducing Poverty

Suppose we tax the rich more heavily—who would get the money, and for what goals?

Reducing poverty, rather than inequality, is also a difficult task, but at least the end is clearer. One new strategy for helping the poor improve their condition is known as the "social impact bond," which is being tested in Britain and has been endorsed by the Obama administration. Under this approach, private investors, including foundations, put up money to pay for a program or initiative to help low-income people get jobs, stay out of prison or remain in school, for example. A government agency evaluates the results. If the program is succeeding, the agency reimburses the investors; if not, they get no government money.

As Harvard economist Jeffrey Liebman has pointed out, for this system to work there must be careful measures of success and a reasonable chance for investors to make a profit. Massachusetts is ready to try such an effort. It may not be easy for the social impact bond model to work consistently, but it offers one big benefit: Instead of carping about who is rich, we would be trying to help people who are poor.

11

Americans Want Less Wealth Inequality than Currently Exists

Michael I. Norton and Dan Ariely

Michael I. Norton is associate professor of business administration and Marvin Bower Fellow at the Harvard Business School and Dan Ariely is the James B. Duke Professor of Psychology and Behavioral Economics at Duke University.

When Americans were asked to estimate the current level of wealth inequality in the United States, they vastly underestimated the wealth owned by the top 20 percent and vastly overestimated the wealth owned by the bottom 40 percent. In addition, when asked what the ideal distribution of wealth was, their preferences were even farther from the current level of wealth inequality, suggesting that Americans favor policies to reduce the wealth gap.

The gap between the wealthiest Americans and the poorest is bigger than at any time since the 1920s—just before the Depression. According to an analysis this year by Edward Wolff of New York University, the top 20% of wealthy individuals own about 85% of the wealth, while the bottom 40% own very near 0%. Many in that bottom 40% not only have no assets, they have negative net wealth.

A gap this pronounced raises the politically divisive question of whether there is a need for wealth redistribution in the United State. This central question underlies such hot-button issues as whether the Bush tax cuts should be allowed to expire and whether the government should provide more assistance to the poor. But before those issues can be addressed, it's important to understand how Americans feel about the country's increasing economic polarity.

Americans' Views on Wealth Inequality

We recently asked a representative sample of more than 5,000 Americans (young and old, men and women, rich and poor, liberal and conservative) to answer two questions. They first were asked to estimate the current level of wealth inequality in the United States, and then they were asked about what they saw as an ideal level of wealth inequality.

In our survey, Americans drastically underestimated the current gap between the very rich and the poor. The typical respondent believed that the top 20% of Americans owned 60% of the wealth, and the bottom 40% owned 10%. They knew, in other words, that wealth in the United States was not distributed equally, but were unaware of just how unequal that distribution was.

To achieve the ideal spelled out by those surveyed, about 50% of the total wealth in the United States would have to be taken from the top 20% and distributed to the remaining 80%.

When we asked respondents to tell us what their ideal distribution of wealth was, things got even more interesting: Americans wanted the top 20% to own just over 30% of the wealth, and the bottom 40% to own about 25%. They still wanted the rich to be richer than the poor, but they wanted the disparity to be much less extreme.

But was there concensus among Americans about their ideal country? Importantly, the answer was an unequivocal "yes." While liberals and the poor favored slightly more equal distributions than conservatives and the wealthy, a large majority of every group we surveyed—from the poorest to the richest, from the most conservative to the most liberal—agreed that the current level of wealth inequality was too high and wanted a more equitable distribution of wealth. In fact, Americans reported wanting to live in a country that looks more like Sweden than the United States.

Policies to Reduce Inequality

So, if Americans say they want a country that is more equal than they believe it to be, and they believe that the country is more equal than it actually is, the question becomes how we lessen these disparities. Our survey didn't ask what measures people would be willing to support to address the wealth gap. But to achieve the ideal spelled out by those surveyed, about 50% of the total wealth in the United States would have to be taken from the top 20% and distributed to the remaining 80%.

Few people would argue for an immediate redistribution of 50% of the nation's wealth, and such a move would unquestionably create chaos. In addition, despite the fact that individual Americans give large amounts to charitable causes each year—in effect, a way of transferring wealth from the rich to the poor—the notion of government redistribution raises hackles among many constituencies.

Despite these reservations, our results suggest that policies that increase inequality—those that favor the wealthy, say, or that place a greater burden on the poor—are unlikely to reflect the desires of Americans from across the political and economic spectrum. Rather, they seem to favor policies that involve taking from the rich and giving to the poor.

12

That Americans Want Less Wealth Inequality Is Irrelevant

Max Borders

Max Borders is editor of The Freeman *magazine and author of* Superwealth: Why We Should Stop Worrying About the "Gap" Between Rich and Poor.

A recent study that purports to show that Americans favor wealth redistribution is flawed in several ways. Polling laypeople about the ideal distribution of wealth is meaningless when divorced from knowledge about the way wealth works. Furthermore, an ideal conception of justice cannot be developed from a simplistic opinion poll. People may have a skewed perception about wealth distribution simply because they actually consider themselves more wealthy than the data would seem to show.

Everyone knows the social sciences are fuzzy. Economists, political scientists, and anthropologists bring their moralistic baggage into the ivory tower as soon as they decide what to study and what not to. Social science is value-laden. But there is baggage and then there is a naked agenda. In the first case you might be a victim of selection bias or other unconscious human processes that cause you to misinterpret your data. In the latter case you simply start with a political agenda along with its (often dubious) premises, and go from there.

A Study Supporting Wealth Redistribution

Michael I. Norton of Harvard and Dan Ariely of Duke fall into the latter category. In a 2010 study, Norton and Ariely appear to be engaging in a kind of democracy-by-proxy. They claim that Americans really want more "wealth redistribution," and they have the evidence to prove it.

Here's their own description of the findings from a *Los Angeles Times* piece, "Spreading the Wealth."

> We recently asked a representative sample of more than 5,000 Americans (young and old, men and women, rich and poor, liberal and conservative) to answer two questions. They first were asked to estimate the current level of wealth inequality in the United States, and then they were asked about what they saw as an ideal level of wealth inequality.
>
> In our survey, Americans drastically underestimated the current gap between the very rich and the poor. The typical respondent believed that the top 20% of Americans owned 60% of the wealth, and the bottom 40% owned 10%. They knew, in other words, that wealth in the United States was not distributed equally, but were unaware of just how unequal that distribution was.
>
> When we asked respondents to tell us what their ideal distribution of wealth was, things got even more interesting: Americans wanted the top 20% to own just over 30% of the wealth, and the bottom 40% to own about 25%. They still wanted the rich to be richer than the poor, but they wanted the disparity to be much less extreme.

Absent any context, the most ardent libertarian surveyed might wish that poor people had more resources and yet not support forced redistribution.

What should we conclude from this? Norton and Ariely did succeed in proving that Americans don't know who has how much money.

Strangely, Norton and Ariely proceed to ask the same Americans who are ignorant about the current wealth distribution what their "ideal" distribution is. Those surveyed then dreamed up what they thought would be a good breakdown, even though no such ideal exists in that great Tablet in the Sky. From all of this surveying, they conclude something that cannot readily be concluded:

> [O]ur results *suggest* that policies that increase inequality— those that favor the wealthy, say, or that place a greater burden on the poor—are unlikely to reflect the desires of Americans from across the political and economic spectrum. Rather, they *seem* to favor policies that involve taking from the rich and giving to the poor. [Emphasis added.]

Notice "suggest" and "seem."

You see, Norton and Ariely can't claim those surveyed favor coercive redistribution. They merely infer it—and in curious fashion. Absent any context, the most ardent libertarian surveyed might wish that poor people had more resources and yet not support forced redistribution. I know I do. But even if they learned most people favor redistribution at some point, we cannot conclude such desires *justify* forced redistribution, much less prove that redistribution is a good thing.

And this is where Norton and Ariely's malpractice really begins.

The Ideal Distribution of Wealth

Academic socialists with bees in their bonnets are eager to point out which quintile has what at every turn, as if concern for the poor somehow automatically translates into worries about the assets of the rich. One reason they do this is they believe laypeople are ignorant: If they were enlightened, they would change their minds and want to alter the distribution.

Somehow, though, this self-same group of distribution-ignorant Americans—when polled about a complete abstraction like the distribution of assets over quintiles—suddenly becomes endowed with a magical insight. Again, Norton and

Ariely want us to think this special insight provides justification for redistributionist policies. But why should we think that Americans factually ignorant in one area would have some sort of mystical authority on the timeless and intractable questions of justice?

In other words, Norton and Ariely conclude that asking Joe Sixpack, Jill Accountant, and Barb Waitress their thoughts about an abstraction like national income quintiles limns some great truth about right, wrong, and the good. Even the venerable soft egalitarian John Rawls would likely have bristled at this, for it is an intrusion into a discipline (philosophy) that demands more than what amounts to the naturalistic fallacy dressed up in finery of Gallup and Zogby.

Ask people for idealized abstractions and you'll get idealized abstractions. After all, aren't people "predictably irrational"?

I wonder: Did any of their respondents have the option of saying, "I don't think there is such an ideal distribution"? To me the whole exercise is as meaningful as asking people what should be the ideal distribution of vehicle types. Suppose for simplicity there are five categories of vehicle: cars, pickups, buses, local trucks, and transfer trucks. Someone with no concept of the function of each vehicle might say each category should have 20 percent of all vehicles—i.e., 20 percent are cars, 20 percent are trucks, 20 percent are buses, and so on. But once we start to think about what each vehicle does, we might conclude that it makes sense for there to be a different, rather unequal, distribution. Similarly, the distribution of assets in quartiles just doesn't tell us anything substantive about the function of wealth (e.g., opportunities, quality of life, upward mobility, or what is likely to make any given person better off). The "ideal distribution" is meaningless because it is completely divorced from much more important questions about the *way wealth works*, which may have much more to do with human well-being than some distribution at some slice in time.

Theories of Justice

Now, speaking of Rawls, Norton and Ariely actually start their paper by claiming their study is Rawlsian: "We take a different approach to determining the 'ideal' level of wealth inequality: Following the philosopher John Rawls (1971), we ask Americans to construct distributions of wealth they deem just." People may have good reasons to disagree with the late Rawls, but his theory is elegant and sophisticated. Norton and Ariely have no business hitching their wagon to Rawls's *A Theory of Justice*.

Rawls's theory was a product of a philosophical reasoning. His theory requires people to think about what sort of society they would want to be born into if they didn't know what their own circumstances would be. Rawls thought people would want a high degree of political freedom, but also security; they would want the least well off to be cared for lest they themselves be born as the least well off. Most importantly, perhaps, Rawls's theory—right or wrong—was a product of philosophical deliberation, not about opinion polls in which people simply come up with a distribution and have academics point to the results as Utopian. So when it comes to Rawls's work, one can only conclude that Norton and Ariely are shrouded in a veil of ignorance.

Norton and Ariely also never consider the possibility that some of their respondents might want to see a different wealth distribution carried out through means other than forced redistribution by the state. For example, might we rid government of all the favor-seeking schemes that protect the assets of banking CEOs [chief executive officers] and agribusiness moguls and shift costs onto the poor and middle class? If people had greater information about the circumstances of time and place—like the effect of taking X dollars from businessman B means B can afford to hire fewer people—would they think differently about matters? Ask people for idealized abstractions and you'll get idealized abstractions. After all, aren't people "predictably irrational"?

If your goal is to alleviate poverty or perhaps to raise the baseline for what constitutes a minimum level of income that would allow most everyone to escape distress, that's something reasonable people can talk about.

Perceptions About Wealth

In his own critique of Norton and Ariely, George Mason University economist Don Boudreaux reminds us that money ain't everything:

> That Americans "drastically" underestimate the wealth of "the very rich" compared to the wealth of "the poor" reveals that the difference in the number of dollars owned by "the very rich" compared to the number of dollars owned by "the poor" translates into a much smaller—that is, far more equal—difference in living standards. In other words, differences in monetary wealth are not the same as differences in living standards.

Indeed, maybe the reason Americans misjudge the actual wealth distribution is that most consider themselves wealthy in Boudreaux's more subjective sense—at least when it comes to the things that matter. (Bill Gates might be able to fly in a private jet, but we can both fly. He might be able to afford $10,000 per-plate caviar, but we can both eat well.) Standard of living is different in important ways from the measure of assets distributed over a population.

As far as "the gap" is concerned, one of the major themes of this book is: *If your goal is to alleviate poverty or perhaps to raise the baseline for what constitutes a minimum level of in-*

come that would allow most everyone to escape distress, that's something reasonable people can talk about.

But that is not the same thing as worrying about what assets the wealthy control.

Suppose you asked the same Americans in the Norton-Ariely study, "If you could guarantee that every poor person in America had their basic needs met, would you agree to abandon your 'ideal' wealth distribution?" Their answers might surprise you. That's because many people conflate the distribution of wealth and concern for the poor. Indeed, we don't find any upper limit on income anywhere in Rawls, either. Rawls's only criterion was that the least advantaged benefit from inequality. If you've ever been to North Korea or Cuba, it's pretty obvious that they do.

13

The Unequal Wealth Created by the Rich Is Essential for the Economy

Richard A. Epstein

Richard A. Epstein is the Laurence A. Tisch Professor of Law at the New York University School of Law.

Wealth inequality in America has its origins in legitimate respect for voluntary ventures and ends up benefitting the system by the increase in overall wealth. Trying to address inequalities of wealth by forced wealth transfer through taxation on the rich will only result in reducing the wealth that is created by the top earners, thus resulting in lower tax revenues and less economic growth.

Taxing the top one percent even more means less wealth and fewer jobs for the rest of us.

The 2008 election was supposed to bring to the United States a higher level of civil discourse. Fast-forward three years and exactly the opposite has happened. A stalled economy brings forth harsh recriminations. As recent polling data reveals, the American public is driven by two irreconcilable emotions. The first is a deep distrust of government, which has driven the approval rate for Congress below ten percent. The second is a strong egalitarian impulse that directs its fury to the top one percent of income earners. Thus the same people who want government to get out of their lives also

Richard A. Epstein, "Three Cheers for Income Inequality." Reprinted from *Defining Ideas*, November 8, 2011, with the permission of the publisher, the Hoover Institution. Copyright © 2011 by the Board of Trustees of the Leland Stanford Junior University.

want government to increase taxes on the rich and corporations. They cannot have it both ways.

I voiced some of my objections to these two points in an interview on PBS, which sparked much controversy. The topic merits much more attention.

Inequality and Economic Prosperity

What are the origins of inequality? Start with a simple world in which all individuals own their labor. Acting in their self-interest (which includes that of family and friends), they seek to improve their lot in life. They cannot use force to advance their own position. Thus, they are left with two alternatives: individual labor and cooperative voluntary ventures.

Voluntary ventures will normally emerge only when all parties to them entertain expectations of gain from entering into these transactions. In some cases, to be sure, these expectations will be dashed. All risky ventures do not pan out. But on average and over time, the few failures cannot derail the many successes. People will make themselves better off.

The successes of the rich afford increased opportunities for gain to other people in the form of new technologies and businesses for others to exploit.

The rub is that they need not do so at even rates. The legitimate origin of the inequality of wealth lies in the simple observation that successful actors outperform unsuccessful ones, without violating their rights. As was said long ago by Justice [Mahlon] Pitney in *Coppage v. Kansas* [1915], "it is from the nature of things impossible to uphold freedom of contract and the right of private property without at the same time recognizing as legitimate those inequalities of fortune that are the necessary result of the exercise of those rights."

So why uphold this combination of property and contract rights? Not because of atavistic fascination for venerable legal institutions. Rather, it is because voluntary exchanges improve overall social welfare. This works in three stages.

First, these transactions, on average, will make all parties to them better off. The only way the rich succeed is by helping their trading partners along the way.

Second, the successes of the rich afford increased opportunities for gain to other people in the form of new technologies and businesses for others to exploit.

Third, the initial success of the rich businessman paves the way for competitors to enter the marketplace. This, in turn, spurs the original businessman to make further improvements to his own goods and services.

In this system, the inequalities in wealth pay for themselves by the vast increases in wealth.

Any defense of wealth inequalities through voluntary means is, however, subject to a powerful caveat: The wealth must be acquired by legitimate means, which do not include aid in the form of state subsidies, state protection, or any other special gimmick. The rich who prosper from these policies do not deserve their wealth. Neither does anyone else who resorts to the same tactics.

As an empirical matter, large businesses, labor unions, and agricultural interests that have profited from government protections have drained huge amounts of wealth from the system. Undoing these protections may or may not change the various indices of inequality. But it will increase the overall size of the pie by improving the overall level of system efficiency.

Redressing Wealth Inequality

The hard question that remains is this: To what extent will the United States, or any other nation, profit by a concerted effort to redress inequalities of wealth?

Again the answer depends on the choice of means. Voluntary forms of redistribution through major charitable foundations pose no threat to the accumulation of wealth. Indeed, they spur its creation by affording additional reasons to acquire levels of wealth that no rational agent could possibly consume.

Forced transfers of wealth through taxation will have the opposite effect. They will destroy the pools of wealth that are needed to generate new ventures, and they will dull the system-wide incentives to create wealth in the first place. There are many reasons for this system-wide failure.

First, the use of state coercion to remedy inequalities of wealth is not easily done. The most obvious method for doing so is by creating subsidies for people at the bottom, which are offset by high rates of taxation for people at the top. The hope is that high taxes will do little to blunt economic activity at the high end, while the payments will do little to dull initiative at the low end.

One reason why the internal revenue code contains such complexity is its desire to combat the private strategies that people, especially those in the top one percent, use to avoid high levels of taxation.

But this program is much more difficult to implement than is commonly supposed. The process of income redistribution opens up opportunities for powerful groups to secure transfers of wealth to themselves. This does nothing to redress inequalities of wealth. Even if these political players are constrained, there is still no costless way to transfer wealth up and down the income scale.

The administrative costs of running a progressive income tax system are legion. Unfortunately, that point was missed in a recent op-ed. Writing in the *New York Times*, Cornell economist Robert H. Frank plumped hard for steeper progressive income tax rates as a way to amend income inequality.

Yet matters are not nearly as simple as he supposes. In his view, the source of complexity in the current income tax code lies in the plethora of special interest provisions that make it difficult to calculate income by recognized standard economic measures. Thus, he thinks that it is "flatly wrong" to think that the flat tax will result in tax simplification. After all, it is just as easy to read a tax schedule that has progressive rates as one that has a uniform flat rate.

The Problems with Progressive Taxation

But more than reading tax schedules is at stake. First, one reason why the internal revenue code contains such complexity is its desire to combat the private strategies that people, especially those in the top one percent, use to avoid high levels of taxation. Anyone who has spent time in dealing with family trusts and partnerships, with income averaging, with the use of real estate shelters, and with foreign investments, knows just how hard it is to protect the progressive rate schedule against manipulation.

Second, the creation of these large tax loopholes is not some act of nature. Frank, like so many defenders of progressive taxation, fails to realize that progressive rates generate huge pressures to create new tax shelters. Lower the overall tax rates and the pressure to create tax gimmicks with real economic costs diminishes. Overall social output is higher with a flat tax than it is with a progressive one.

Third, the dangers posed by the use of progressive taxation are not confined to these serious administrative issues. There are also larger questions of political economy at stake. The initial question is just how steep the progressive tax ought to be.

Keep it too shallow, and it does little to generate additional public revenues to justify the added cost of administration. Make it too steep, and it will reduce the incentives to create wealth that are always unambiguously stronger under a flat tax system. But since no one knows the optimal level of progressivity, vast quantities of wealth are dissipated in fighting over these levels. The flat tax removes that dimension of political intrigue.

The inefficiencies created by a wide range of tax and business initiatives reduces the wealth earned by people in that top one percent, and thus the tax base on which the entire redistributive state depends.

Fourth, sooner or later—and probably sooner—high tax rates will kill growth. Progressives like Frank operate on the assumption that high taxation rates have little effect on investment by asking whether anyone would quit a cushy job just to save a few tax dollars. But the situation is in reality far more complex. One key to success in the United States lies in its ability to attract foreign labor and foreign capital to our shores. In this we are in competition with other nations whose tax policies are far more favorable to new investment than ours. The loss of foreign people and foreign capital is not easy to observe because we cannot identify with certainty most of the individuals who decide to go elsewhere. But we should at the very least note that there is the risk of a brain drain as the best and brightest foreign workers who came to the United States in search of economic opportunity ultimately may return home. They will likely not want to brave the hostile business climate that they see in the United States.

Fifth, sophisticated forms of tax avoidance are not limited to foreign laborers. Rich people have a choice of tax-free and taxable investments. They can increase transfers to family members in order to reduce the incidence of high progressive taxation. They can retire a year sooner, or go part-time to reduce their tax burdens. And of course, they can fight the incidence of higher taxation by using their not inconsiderable influence in the tax arenas.

Sixth, the inefficiencies created by a wide range of tax and business initiatives reduces the wealth earned by people in that top one percent, and thus the tax base on which the entire redistributive state depends. Defenders of progressive taxation, like Frank, cite the recent report of the Congressional Budget Office [CBO], which shows huge increases of wealth in the top one percent from 1979 to 2007. The top one percent increased its wealth by 275 percent in those years. The rest of the income distribution lagged far behind.

Unfortunately, the CBO report was out of date the day it was published. We now have tax data available that runs through 2009, which shows the folly of seeking to rely on heavier rates of taxation on the top one percent. The Tax Foundation's October 24, 2011 report, contains this solemn reminder of the risks of soaking the rich in bad times:

> In 2009, the top 1 percent of tax returns paid 36.7 percent of all federal individual income taxes and earned 16.9 percent of adjusted gross income (AGI), compared to 2008 when those figures were 38.0 percent and 20.0 percent, respectively. Both of those figures—share of income and share of taxes paid—were their lowest since 2003 when the top 1 percent earned 16.7 percent of adjusted gross income and paid 34.3 percent of federal individual income taxes.

It is worth adding that the income of the top one percent also dropped 20 percent between 2007 and 2008, with a concomitant loss in tax revenues.

The Danger of Punishing High Earners

There are several disturbing implications that flow from this report. The first is that these figures explain the vulnerability in bad times of our strong dependence on high-income people to fund the transfer system. The current contraction in wealth at the top took place with only few new taxes. The decline in taxable income at the top will only shrink further if tax rates are raised. A mistake, therefore, in setting tax rate increases could easily wreck the entire system. Indeed, the worst possible outcome would be for high taxation to lower top incomes drastically. Right now, for better or worse, the entire transfer system of the United States is dependent on the continued success of high-income earners whom the egalitarians would like to punish.

The United States is now in the midst of killing the goose that lays the golden eggs.

Put otherwise, if a person at the middle of the income distribution loses a dollar in income, the federal government loses nothing in income tax revenues. Let a rich person suffer that decline and the revenue loss at the federal level is close to 40 percent, with more losses at the state level. The slow growth policies of the last three years have cost far more in revenue from the top one percent than any increase in progressive taxation could possibly hope to achieve. The more we move toward an equal income policy, the more we shall need tax increases on the middle class to offset the huge revenue losses at the top. Our current political economy makes the bottom 99 percent hostage to the continued success of the rich.

The dangers of the current obsession with income inequality should be clear. The rhetorical excesses of people like Robert Frank make it ever easier to champion a combination of high taxation schemes coupled with ever more stringent regulations of labor and capital markets. Together, these schemes spell the end of the huge paydays of the top one percent. Those earners depend heavily on a growth in asset value, which is just not happening today.

But what about the flat tax? Frank and others are right to note that a return to the flat tax will result in an enormous redistribution of income to the top one percent from everyone else. But why assume that the current level of progressivity sets the legitimate baseline, especially in light of the current anemic levels of economic growth? What theory justifies progressive taxation in the first place? The current system presupposes that this nation can continue to fund the aspirations of 99 percent out of the wealth of the one percent. That will prove to be unsustainable. A return to a flatter tax (ideally a flat) tax will have just the short-term consequences that Frank fears. It will undo today's massively redistributivist policies. But it will also go a long way toward unleashing growth in our heavily regulated and taxed economy.

The United States is now in the midst of killing the goose that lays the golden eggs. That current strategy is failing in the face of economic stagnation, even with no increase in tax rates. It will quickly crumble if tax increases are used to feed the current coalition of unions and farmers who will receive much of the revenue, while the employment prospects of ordinary people languish for want of the major capital investments that often depend on the wealth of the privileged one percent of the population.

The clarion call for more income equality puts short-term transfers ahead of long-term growth. Notwithstanding the temper of the times, that siren call should be stoutly resisted. Enterprise and growth, not envy and stagnation, are the keys to economic revival.

Organizations to Contact

The editors have compiled the following list of organizations concerned with the issues debated in this book. The descriptions are derived from materials provided by the organizations. All have publications or information available for interested readers. The list was compiled on the date of publication of the present volume; the information provided here may change. Be aware that many organizations take several weeks or longer to respond to inquiries, so allow as much time as possible.

American Enterprise Institute for Public Policy Research (AEI)
1150 17th St. NW, Washington, DC   20036
(202) 862-5800 • fax: (202) 862-7177
e-mail: info@aei.org
website: www.aei.org

The American Enterprise Institute for Public Policy Research (AEI) is a private, nonpartisan, nonprofit institution dedicated to research and education on issues of government, politics, economics, and social welfare. AEI sponsors research and publishes materials aimed at defending the principles and improving the institutions of American freedom and democratic capitalism. Among AEI's publications is the online magazine, *The American*, and the book *Prices, Poverty, and Inequality: Why Americans Are Better Off than You Think*.

American Federation of Labor and Congress of Industrial Organizations (AFL-CIO)
815 16th St. NW, Washington, DC   20006
(202) 637-5000
website: www.aflcio.org

The American Federation of Labor and Congress of Industrial Organizations (AFL-CIO) is a voluntary federation of fifty-six national and international labor unions, representing 12.2

million members. The AFL-CIO educates union members about issues that affect the daily lives of working families and encourages them to make their voice heard by government. The AFL-CIO has numerous publications available at its website concerning wealth and income distribution in the United States, including "Working America: Wealth Inequality Is Much Worse Than You Think (and Congress Just Made It Worse)."

Cato Institute

1000 Massachusetts Ave. NW, Washington, DC 20001-5403
(202) 842-0200 • fax: (202) 842-3490
website: www.cato.org

The Cato Institute is a public policy research foundation dedicated to the principles of individual liberty, limited government, free markets, and peace. Its scholars and analysts conduct independent, nonpartisan research on a wide range of policy issues. Among its publications are the quarterly journal of public policy analysis, *Cato Journal*; the bimonthly *Cato Policy Report*; and *Policy Analysis* articles such as "Thinking Clearly About Economic Inequality."

Center for American Progress

1333 H St. NW, 10th Floor, Washington, DC 20005
(202) 682-1611 • fax: (202) 682-1867
website: www.americanprogress.org

The Center for American Progress is a nonprofit, nonpartisan organization dedicated to improving the lives of Americans through progressive ideas and action. The Center for American Progress dialogues with leaders, thinkers, and citizens to explore the vital issues facing America and the world. The Center publishes numerous research papers, which are available at its website, including, "The Impact of Inequality on Growth."

Center for Economic and Policy Research (CEPR)

1611 Connecticut Ave. NW, Suite 400, Washington, DC 20009
(202) 293-5380 • fax: (202) 588-1356

e-mail: cepr@cepr.net
website: www.cepr.net

The Center for Economic and Policy Research (CEPR) aims to promote democratic debate on the most important economic and social issues that affect people's lives. CEPR conducts both professional research and public education. The organization also provides briefings and testimony to Congress and reports for the general public, including "Inequality as Policy: The United States Since 1979."

Center on Budget and Policy Priorities (CBPP)
820 First St. NE, Suite 510, Washington, DC   20002
(202) 408-1080 • fax: (202) 408-1056
e-mail: center@cbpp.org
website: www.cbpp.org

The Center on Budget and Policy Priorities (CBPP) is a policy organization working at the federal and state levels on fiscal policy and public programs that affect low- and moderate-income families and individuals. CBPP conducts research and analysis to inform public debates over proposed budget and tax policies, developing policy options to alleviate poverty. There are many reports available at CBPP's website, including "A Guide to Statistics on Historical Trends in Income Inequality."

Economic Policy Institute (EPI)
1333 H St. NW, Suite 300, East Tower
Washington, DC   20005-4707
(202) 775-8810 • fax: (202) 775-0819
e-mail: epi@epi.org
website: www.epi.org

The Economic Policy Institute (EPI) is a nonprofit think tank that seeks to broaden the discussion about economic policy to include the interests of low- and middle-income workers. EPI briefs policy makers at all levels of government; provides technical support to national, state, and local activists and community organizations; testifies before national, state, and local legislatures; and provides information and background to the print and electronic media. EPI publishes books, studies, issue briefs, popular education materials, and other resources, among which is its flagship publication, *The State of Working America*, the full text of which is available online.

Institute for Women's Policy Research (IWPR)
1200 18th St. NW, Suite 301, Washington, DC   20036
(202) 785-5100 • fax: (202) 833-4362
e-mail: iwpr@iwpr.org
website: www.iwpr.org

The Institute for Women's Policy Research (IWPR) conducts research and disseminates its findings to address the needs of women, promote public dialog, and strengthen families, communities, and societies. With initiatives on the topics of education, democracy, poverty, work, and health, IWPR aims to promote gender equity. IWPR publishes numerous reports and briefing papers, including "Pay Secrecy and Wage Discrimination."

United for a Fair Economy (UFE)
1 Milk St., 5th Floor, Boston, MA   02109
(617) 423-2148 • fax: (617) 423-0191
e-mail: info@faireconomy.org
website: www.faireconomy.org

United for a Fair Economy (UFE) aims to raise awareness that concentrated wealth and power undermine the economy, corrupt democracy, deepen the racial divide, and tear communities apart. UFE supports and helps build social movements for greater equality through such projects as its Racial Wealth Divide program. UFE has numerous resources available at its website, including reports and infographics.

Urban Institute
2100 M St. NW, Washington, DC   20037
(202) 833-7200
website: www.urban.org

The Urban Institute works to foster sound public policy and effective government by gathering data, conducting research, evaluating programs, and educating Americans on social and economic issues. The Urban Institute builds knowledge about the nation's social and fiscal challenges through evidence-based research meant to diagnose problems and figure out which policies and programs work best, for whom, and how. The Institute publishes policy briefs, commentary, and research reports, including "Less Than Equal: Racial Disparities in Wealth Accumulation."

Bibliography

Books

Orazio P. Attanasio, Erich Battistin, and Mario Padula — *Inequality in Living Standards Since 1980*. Washington, DC: AEI Press, 2010.

Francine D. Blau — *Gender, Inequality, and Wages*. New York: Oxford University Press, 2012.

Chuck Collins — *99 to 1: How Wealth Inequality Is Wrecking the World and What We Can Do About It*. San Francisco: Berrett-Koehler Publishers, 2012.

Uri Dadush et al. — *Inequality in America*. Washington, DC: Brookings Institution Press, 2012.

Peter Edelman — *So Rich, So Poor: Why It's So Hard to End Poverty in America*. New York: New Press, 2012.

Howard Steven Friedman — *The Measure of a Nation: How to Regain America's Competitive Edge and Boost Our Global Standing*. Amherst, NY: Prometheus Books, 2012.

Diana Furchtgott-Roth — *Women's Figures: An Illustrated Guide to the Economic Progress of Women in America*. Washington, DC: AEI Press, 2012.

Jacob Hacker and Paul Pierson	*Winner-Take-All Politics: How Washington Made the Rich Richer and Turned Its Back on the Middle Class.* New York: Simon & Schuster, 2010.
Leslie McCall	*The Undeserving Rich: American Beliefs About Inequality, Opportunity, and Redistribution.* New York: Cambridge University Press, 2013.
Timothy Noah	*The Great Divergence: America's Growing Inequality Crisis and What We Can Do About It.* New York: Bloomsbury Press, 2012.
Benjamin I. Page and Lawrence R. Jacobs	*Class War? What Americans Really Think About Economic Inequality.* Chicago: University of Chicago Press, 2009.
Robert B. Reich	*Aftershock: The Next Economy and America's Future.* New York: Vintage Books, 2011.
Tavis Smiley and Cornel West	*The Rich and the Rest of Us: A Poverty Manifesto.* New York: Smiley Books, 2012.
Joseph Stiglitz	*The Price of Inequality: How Today's Divided Society Endangers Our Future.* New York: W.W. Norton, 2012.
Richard Wilkinson and Kate Pickett	*The Spirit Level: Why Greater Equality Makes Societies Stronger.* New York: Bloomsbury Press, 2010.

Periodicals and Internet Sources

Jared Bernstein — "The Impact of Inequality on Growth," Center for American Progress, December 2013. www.americanprogress.org.

Donald J. Boudreaux and Mark J. Perry — "The Myth of a Stagnant Middle Class," *Wall Street Journal*, January 23, 2013.

Jamelle Bouie — "The Titanic Wealth Gap Between Blacks and Whites," *American Prospect*, February 27, 2013. www.prospect.org.

Steve Conover — "The Myth of Middle-Class Stagnation," *American*, September 16, 2011. www.american.com.

Peter Ferrara — "Obama's Rising Inequality," *American Spectator*, May 8, 2013. www.spectator.org.

Ron Haskins — "The Myth of the Disappearing Middle Class," *Washington Post*, March 29, 2012.

Ariane Hegewisch, Claudia Williams, and Angela Edwards — "The Gender Wage Gap: 2012," Institute for Women's Policy Research, March 2013 www.iwpr.org.

Richard W. Johnson and Janice S. Park — "Employment and Earnings Among 50+ People of Color," *Retirement Security Data Brief*, August 2011. www.urban.org.

Rakesh Kochhar, Richard Fry, and Paul Taylor	"Wealth Gaps Rise to Record Highs Between Whites, Blacks, Hispanics," Pew Research Center, July 26, 2011. www.pewsocialtrends.org.
Stewart Lansley	"The Hourglass Society," *Los Angeles Review of Books*, May 28, 2013. www.lareviewofbooks.org.
Steven J. Markovich	"The Income Inequality Debate," Council on Foreign Relations, September 2012. www.cfr.org.
Signe-Mary McKernan et al.	"Less than Equal: Racial Disparities in Wealth Accumulation," Urban Institute, April 2013. www.urban.org.
Charles Murray	"The New American Divide," *Wall Street Journal*, January 23, 2012.
Timothy Noah	"The United States of Inequality, Entry 10: Why We Can't Ignore Growing Income Inequality," *Slate*, September 3, 2010. www.slate.com.
Pew Social & Demographic Trends	"Fewer, Poorer, Gloomier: The Lost Decade of the Middle Class," Pew Research Center, August 22, 2012. www.pewsocialtrends.org.
Alan Reynolds	"Tax Rates, Inequality and the 1%," *Wall Street Journal*, December 6, 2011.
John Schmitt	"Inequality as Policy: The United States Since 1979," Center for Economic and Policy Research (CEPR), October 2009. www.cepr.net.

Thomas Shapiro, Tatjana Meschede, and Sam Osoro	"The Roots of the Widening Racial Wealth Gap: Explaining the Black-White Economic Divide," Institute on Assets and Social Policy, February 2013. www.iasp.brandeis.edu.
Dustin Siggins	"Wealth and Inequality on YouTube," *National Review Online*, March 27, 2013. www.nationalreview.com.
John Stossel	"Making Life Fair," *Reason*, May 17, 2012. www.reason.com.
Derek Thompson	"Wealth Inequality Is a Problem, but How Do You Even Begin to Solve It?," *Atlantic*, March 6, 2013.
Jordan Weissmann	"US Income Inequality: It's Worse Today than It Was in 1774," *Atlantic*, September 19, 2012.
Will Wilkinson	"Thinking Clearly About Economic Inequality," *Policy Analysis*, no. 640, July 14, 2009. www.cato.org.
Scott Winship	"Overstating the Costs of Inequality," *National Affairs*, Spring 2013.
Michael D. Yates	"The Great Inequality," *Monthly Review*, March 2012.

Index